DRINK
FROM THE
RIVER
OF
DELIGHT

Welcome to God's Healing
Space in His Word

JANET S. ABADIR MD

Isaiah 61 Publishing
PO Box 8043
Kodiak AK 99615
Copyright © 2024 by Janet Abadir

Print ISBN: 978-1-966338-00-0
Digital ISBN: 978-1-966338-01-7

Thank you for your purchase of this book.

For a free study guide, please visit JanetAbadir.com

To my Dad, Sami A.M. Abadir, MD

Thank you for your courage, love, and faith. I am who I am today because of you by the grace of God.

Your life was a song, revealing God's majesty and faithfulness. Your praise to Him in every difficult circumstance remains my inspiration. The hymns in this book are among your favorites.

Today, when I drink from the river of delight, I picture you face-to-face with Jesus, enjoying every moment. When I sing at church, I picture myself next to you around the throne of God saying, "Holy, holy, holy, is the Lord God Almighty, who was and is and is to come!"

I love you, Dad, and I miss you every day. You will always be a blessing to me.

Table of Contents

Introduction...11

Chapter 1: You are Thirstier Than You Know...........................17

Chapter 2: Find Delight in the Bible 27

Chapter 3: The Dry Riverbed of Perfectionism 33

Chapter 4: How to Drink from the River...................................41

Chapter 5: How Drinking from the River Moves Us from Offense
to Honor 51

Chapter 6: Delight in Winning..59

Chapter 7: Motivation to Drink Deeply from the River 67

Chapter 8: Delight in the Fear of the Lord................................73

Chapter 9: Abundant Life in the Body of Christ 81

Chapter 10: Fight Sin with the Gospel......................................95

Chapter 11: Treasure your Treasure 105

Chapter 12: Glory and Rest in Jesus.......................................113

Epilogue 121

Personal Notes 127

Acknowledgments...129

Introduction

Every moment of our existence is a fight for space.

I've seen the results of many car accidents as a trauma surgeon. Two or more objects try to occupy the same space at the same time resulting in massive damage and sometimes death. Similarly, all relationships are like a dance where we come close to each other's space without stepping on toes or overpowering. Survival in the world and in relationships depends on maintaining your physical and emotional space. Without space, we are trapped, suffocated, and crushed.

Suffering in our lives is like a crushing weight. Grief overwhelms and presses down on us. Traumatic events take away our breath of hope and joy. A relationship or circumstance can easily trap us and narrow our view or limit our options. Life inevitably brings us to places we would rather not go, or harms something precious to us.

This has been my experience lately. My space has been invaded. My foundations and assumptions about life have been shaken like an earthquake. My dad passed away suddenly, my job exploded in my hands, and I find myself pinned beneath a rock and a hard place. Anxiety wells up quickly, with its accomplices hopelessness and depression.

I need a safe space, a healing space, and divine assistance. I need God's rescue.

God has been graciously speaking to me this year through His Word, the Bible. King David wrote these words about three thousand years ago, giving us hope and healing spaces:

> "[God] sent from on high, he took me; he drew me out of many waters. He rescued me from my strong enemy and from those who hated me, for they were too mighty for me. They confronted me on the day of my calamity, but the LORD was my support. He brought me out into a broad place; he rescued me, because he delighted in me" (Psalm 18:16-19).

We need to know there is a safe space for us when we are pressed on every side. God welcomes us with open arms. He delights in us. He rescues us. He does this as many times as we need. How do we absolutely know this is true? Because of Jesus, who was crushed for our sake so we could be rescued. He was pressed down into death and judgment by the wrath of God, losing His space so we could have a place of honor for eternity. His resurrection guarantees that we belong in the family of God forever.

The purpose of this book is to show you the way I have found to the only safe space of healing. God offers us His trustworthy Word to guide us there. He can heal anything and anyone, because He is Jehovah-Rapha, the LORD our healer (Exodus 15:26). As you follow Jesus, your life will be uncrushable, full of freedom and infinite love. All you need for this journey is faith in the God of the Bible. Unshakable faith, built on the firm foundation of Christ, is God's will for your life. He wants your life to radiate the beauty of Christ, and to be effective in His kingdom. He welcomes you and uses all circumstances for His glory and for your good. What an eternal purpose we have in Christ, and what confidence we have in God's ultimate success and victory!

I have practiced medicine for twenty-four years, and I have met many people who profess to know Jesus Christ, and yet their lives lack power, transformation, and authenticity. I have heard people say, "I tried Christianity, and it didn't work for me." I know many Christians who miss out on connecting with God through His Word. I have experienced times in my own life when my faith did not seem to meet my needs. I felt lonely, starving, and desperate, even though I claimed to know God. My suffering would overwhelm me, leading to worry and defensive behavior instead of faith and trust in God.

This book will show you truths from the Bible that can help you in any suffering. You will see how to experience life to the fullest: life in relationship with God. This goes beyond religious fluff, beyond going through the motions. God wants His people to be fully engaged with Him.

God is looking for people who will worship Him alone, in spirit and in truth (John 4:23). Are you hoping to be one of those people too? Would you like to drink deeply from the river of delights, feasting on the abundance of God's house (Psalm 36:8)?

The great news I want to share with you is that God is willing and able to do this in your life and mine! On December 5,

2023, my job as a rural general surgeon exploded in my hands and left me wondering what to do with myself after pursuing and practicing medicine for my entire adult life. That same night, my town of Kodiak, Alaska, experienced a powerful windstorm which shook my house and kept me from sleeping. I felt God speaking to me as I laid in my bed.

He said, "Janet, this is the storm that would have blown the roof off of your house had I not intervened." I remembered all God's mighty interventions, allowing us to purchase the house "as is" after renting it for nine years, and finish extensive roof repairs. My husband and kids and I had prayed for God to help us, and we had seen His mighty hand of provision again and again. My humble response, "Yes Lord, thank you!" His reply: "So why are you worried about a job?" In my heart I knew that He would take care of me, but I also knew He wanted me to trust Him in this moment.

And so began my next phase of this journey towards healing. I felt I had more questions than answers. Would I crumble under the storm? Would my foundation hold? Who am I if not a practicing surgeon? What resources do I have to draw from in this crisis? What does God offer me in this moment?

God's answer to me was that He was there all along. He is the God Who Sees: 'El Roi' (Genesis 16:13). He gave me an awareness of His presence and love that carries me along every day. I hope you learn to experience His presence as well, enjoying His goodness, love, and faithfulness.

I want to show you that God is real, active, and worthy of our unconditional trust. He delights in us, His children. He is an ever-present help in trouble. I pray you will see the glory of God as you read my story, and dig into God's Word, and that your heart will be moved to worship, wonder, and joy. I pray He shows you the way to His place of healing and hope in Christ. God is in the business of redeeming broken vessels, transforming lives, and creating beauty, and He wants to do it in you! As you start to see this pattern in the Bible, you will see it in your life as well. You are now part of God's story when you believe in Jesus.

I am writing out of what I have learned in my struggle and the treasure I have found in Jesus. I can tell you with certainty it is all worth it. Your faith will grow as you spend time in His Word, marinating in the truths of the gospel. The two questions answered in this book are: how do you get what you need from reading the Bible, and how do you get to the safe, healing space God offers.

Please read the Bible passages quoted in this book when you start and after you finish each chapter. Ask God to speak to you as you read the verses. He is speaking to you right now! Ask Him to help you listen.

CHAPTER 1:

You are Thirstier Than You Know:
Only One Place to Go

"Then a demon-oppressed man who was blind and mute was brought to [Jesus], and he healed him, so that the man spoke and saw. And all the people were amazed, and said, 'Can this man be the Son of David?' But when the Pharisees heard it, they said, 'It is only by Beelzebul, the prince of demons, that this man casts out demons.' Knowing their thoughts, he said to them, 'Every kingdom divided against itself is laid waste, and no city or house divided against itself will stand. And if Satan casts out Satan, he is divided against himself. How then will his kingdom stand? And if I cast out demons by Beelzebul, by whom do your sons cast them out? Therefore they will be your judges. But if it is by the Spirit of God that I cast out demons, then the kingdom of God has come upon you. Or how can someone enter a strong man's house and plunder his goods, unless he first binds the strong man? Then indeed he may plunder his house. Whoever is not with me is against me, and whoever does not gather with me scatters. Therefore I tell you, every sin and blasphemy will be forgiven people, but the blasphemy against the Spirit will

not be forgiven. And whoever speaks a word against the
Son of Man will be forgiven, but whoever speaks against
the Holy Spirit will not be forgiven, either in this age or in
the age to come.'"
- Matthew 12:22-32

"Today, if you hear his voice, do not harden your hearts."
- Psalm 95:7-8

Do you feel alive today?

If you are reading this book, then you are alive. Your body is
working. Your heart is beating, blood is flowing, your brain is
processing electrical signals. Your digestive system is moving
your last meal through and extracting energy and nutrients.
Your lungs are expanding and deflating as you take a few deep
breaths, settling into this chapter. Your body really is quite a
complicated machine. As a doctor, I am so thankful when bodies are working well.

But obviously, that is not the answer I was waiting to hear.
Feeling alive is very different from *being* alive. Feeling alive
is all about connection. It's about being connected to this moment, to your sensations, to people, to the spiritual realm, and
to your life's story and purpose. Positive emotions such as joy,
delight, and pleasure, can enhance your feelings about your
life. This book is about experiencing delight and reconnecting
to true life which is flowing from God to you. When you experience how satisfying it is to be connected to God, you realize
you have been thirsty for Him all your life.

Next question: Are you in control of your emotions?

You may think this is a simple question, but there is a whole lot more behind your emotional state than meets the eye. Intense emotional response can quickly take over our conscious state. Our "fight, flight, or freeze" nervous system is activated by stress and threats, and results in bursts of hormones which affect our entire body. These hormones are powerful, and we do not control them with our reasoning mind.

Sometimes emotions can be so strong they are unavoidable. To be human is to experience emotions, but we realize that a human controlled only by emotions is very unstable. As a surgeon, I learned to suppress my emotions, and to compartmentalize. I might be telling someone they have a deadly cancer, then immediately compose myself to help my next patient with appendicitis. Sometimes it would be days later that I would experience the sorrow and grief of what I had seen.

The spiritual realm can also affect our emotions. Matthew 12:22 describes a man so oppressed by demons that he could not see or speak. There are indeed invisible spiritual forces which can influence us, whether we believe in them or not. When I was studying abroad for a semester in France, I traveled to a former German concentration camp in Dachau, Germany. My emotional state was overwhelmed and oppressed for days after my visit. The evil that had occurred there still had lasting spiritual effects more than fifty years later.

I have been trained as a surgeon to ignore my emotional response to stress and trauma so I can think clearly in high stakes environments. No one wants their surgeon to collapse in tears on the ground when they roll into the emergency room after a car accident. If someone is bleeding to death, dying of an infection, or experiencing excruciating pain, their caregivers must stay calm and remember their training. Panic is not an option.

But what happens when panic is all you can do? How can you function? I have been experiencing so much stress and panic this year that even with all my training and practice, I feel like I cannot escape. It's the sensation of feeling trapped, cornered, and crushed. I just want to run away, but I cannot. I have tried breathing exercises, tapping, counseling, diet, and exercise, with lackluster results. I need a healing space, a broad space, a safe space where I can find freedom.

Jesus offers us that space today.

What do I mean by space? Space is a general term with many meanings. Space can be physical like the space your body is occupying right now. Space can be emotional when you experience and process your environment without coercion or fear. Space exists in the spiritual realm when you are free from demonic oppression and influence. Space exists in relationships when there is no abuse or manipulation or enslavement. When things are hard, I want to run to my safe space, such as my home with my family, or out in nature on a hike or kayak.

You may have heard the psychological terms, "holding space," and "boundaries" in relationships. Holding space means to listen to someone else with your full attention and empathy but withholding judgment or even advice. Boundaries are property lines. In relationships, you learn so much by just defining what is your property, and what belongs to someone else.

How does this help me today when I am overwhelmed by my feelings of anxiety and panic? When hardships invade my space, taking over my property, I have a safe place to run.

In the passage above, Jesus says that He has invaded this world and has bound up the strong man, Satan. What we do not realize is that we were born into slavery to Satan because of sin. In Genesis 3, when Adam and Eve sinned in the Garden of Eden, their allegiance changed. God was their friend, but they rejected Him and made an alliance with Satan when they acted on and believed his lies.

Ever since then, all humans have lived in a state of enmity with God because of their sin nature and rebellion. Now Jesus is seeking and saving the lost and enslaved. We can belong to Jesus. Satan's kingdom is one of mute and blind people who are enslaved to a cruel and wicked master. Jesus wants to plunder Satan's goods by rescuing us out of Satan's kingdom and transferring us to His kingdom. Jesus' kingdom is eternal, safe, and happy beyond belief.

I am so thirsty for this kingdom, this river of delight flowing for me. I want to drink deeply, knowing that God's river will never run dry because He is our infinite source. Eden in Hebrew means "delight." Paradise and delight were lost in the fall of mankind, but the Bible shows us God's way back to delight. I am powerless to get there by myself, just like the mute and blind man. In my oppression, others must help me and bring me to Jesus for healing. I am like the Pharisees, naturally doubting Jesus' power and questioning His authority. Yet I see that the Holy Spirit is working and speaking to my heart—and to yours—if we will listen.

Jesus is so welcoming to those who know they do not have enough power. It's the people who think they are strong who cannot enjoy Jesus. Grace is the unmerited favor and blessing of God, and the only prerequisite is need. The kingdom of God is upside down: the humble, weak, and needy receive it. The proud and the self-sufficient do not. The astounding truth is that God chooses and calls people to know Him even while we were His enemies (Romans 5:8). He wants us in His kingdom, and He invites us to surrender our enmity and accept His friendship. Our allegiance can change by the grace of God.

This passage in Matthew has alarmed and confused readers because of the terrifying and permanent effects of blasphemy against the Holy Spirit. Jesus is making us choose between two options. Either we accept what the Holy Spirit is telling us today and we allow God to change our heart, or we belong to the other kingdom, the kingdom of this world and Satan. The two kingdoms are at war with each other and there will be no truce. One day Satan will be defeated, and the kingdom of this world will become the kingdom of our Lord and of His Christ, and He shall reign forever and ever (Revelation 11:15).

The people around Jesus were wondering if He could be the Son of David. This is an example of the Bible being one cohesive story, the true Word of God. The good news of the Bible is summed up in the first book, in this verse, Genesis 3:15: "I [God] will put enmity between you [Satan] and the woman, and between your offspring and her offspring; he shall bruise your head, and you shall bruise his heel." This is the beginning of the story: God's good world has been invaded by the evil Satan and he is out to destroy mankind. God is sending a Savior, a Messiah, a Chosen One who will destroy Satan after being wounded in the battle. This Man is the seed of the woman. In 2 Samuel 7 we see that this Man will also come from King David's line, and He will reign forever. Jesus gives us evidence in this story that He is indeed the Son of David: He knows people's thoughts and He reacts humbly to the opposition of the Pharisees. He understands that we are slow to believe, and He offers us grace and forgiveness, and an invitation to be a part of His kingdom, with the warning that someday it may be too late to join Him.

Have you experienced the crushing weight of sin, death, and Satan's oppression? Do you want to be rescued by Jesus? Do you long to live in the abundant kingdom of God, drinking from the river of delight every day? What a gift Jesus offers us: to have true sight, words of life to speak, and freedom from the control of demonic influences. The kingdom of God has started already because Jesus has come and bound the strong man by dying on the cross. We will see Jesus return in the future, claim the earth for His own, and throw Satan into Hell, but for now we live in this in between time where faith is needed to see these hidden truths.

God's kingdom is what I am pursing with my whole heart. I have seen the power of God in my life, restoring my vitality and connection and purpose. The Holy Spirit is at work in me, bringing me back to Jesus every time I need Him. He faithfully reminds me that He is with me, and He is the author of my story. When my heart is quietly trusting Him, humble and surrendered, He speaks to me. I pray the same for you today.

As we come to Jesus in humble dependence, He sees us, rescues us, and changes us. He can remove the spirit of anxiety, discouragement, and panic from us. Let the word of God and the Holy Spirit speak to your heart today. Today if you hear His voice, do not harden your heart. The way to your heart is through your ears, so listen carefully. God is speaking and inviting you in. You are welcome to drink to your heart's delight.

Take a few deep breaths and picture yourself drinking in this life and delight that Jesus is offering to you today. Go back and read the verses again and ask God to show you these truths.

Come Ye Sinners, Poor and Needy by Joseph Hart

Come ye sinners, poor and needy, weak and wounded, sick and sore;
Jesus ready stands to save you, full of pity, love and pow'r.

Come ye thirsty, come and welcome, God's free bounty glorify;
true belief and true repentance, every grace that brings you nigh.

Let not conscience make you linger, nor of fitness fondly dream;
all the fitness He requireth is to feel your need of Him.

Come ye weary, heavy laden, lost and ruined by the fall;
if you tarry till you're better, you will never come at all.

Lo! th'incarnate God, ascended, pleads the merit of His blood;
venture on Him, venture wholly; let no other trust intrude.

CHAPTER 2:

Find Delight in the Bible:
Jesus is the Word Made Flesh

"Some were fools through their sinful ways, and because of their iniquities suffered affliction; they loathed any kind of food, and they drew near to the gates of death. Then they cried to the LORD in their trouble, and he delivered them from their distress. He sent out his word and healed them and delivered them from their destruction. Let them thank the LORD for his steadfast love, for his wondrous works to the children of man!"
- Psalm 107:17-22

"How sweet are your words to my taste, sweeter than honey to my mouth!"
- Psalm 119:103

"And the Word became flesh and dwelt among us, and we have seen his glory, glory as of the only Son from the Father, full of grace and truth."
- John 1:14

All of us choose not to question something. We must build our lives on one truth that we will not question. Tim Keller writes,

"Our culture tells us to submit everything to our understanding, to question everything including the Bible. But everyone must choose something to not question. Modern people don't question their right and ability to question everything. So everyone is living by faith in some ultimate authority. [The Bible] calls us to make it God's Word, not our reason and intuition."[1]

What is this unquestionable truth for you? How should we relate to God's authority? Is it good to question God?

In the Bible, this is called "testing God," and it is not a virtue (Psalm 95:7-9). God desires faith and trust in His people. As Hebrews 11:6 says, "And without faith it is impossible to please him, for whoever would draw near to God must believe that he exists and that he rewards those who seek him."

I have learned that my study of the Bible is completely different when I come to the Bible humbly, meekly, and obediently, ready to hear what God will say. He is God, and therefore I cannot comprehend Him with my human, finite mind. Do I say to myself, "I could never believe in a God who would do…" or do I say, "You know best, God, and I will trust You no matter what." This prayer is the key to finding delight in reading the Word.

The Bible is a supernatural book, the Word of God. Think of the creation account in Genesis 1. Every time God wanted to create something, He spoke, and it happened. He is the immutable, unchanging God, so anytime He wants to create faith in you—or peace, or wisdom—He speaks, but this time in the form of the written word. Think of the power you hold in your

---

1 Tim Keller, *God's Wisdom for Navigating Life* (New York: Viking, 2017), 23.

hands when you hold the Bible. This is the living, active word of God, ready to reveal your heart, teach you about the eternal God, and transform your life! Why do so many Christians let their Bibles get dusty next to their beds?

I hope to show you some life-transforming truths from the Bible and help you know our Savior better. But none of these techniques will work unless you give up your "right" to invent your own version of God. A made-up "god" is not all-powerful. A made-up "god" is not sovereign. A made-up "god" cannot rescue you.

The bad news is, the real God of the Bible will offend you. He will stretch you. He may cause suffering to transform you. He is going to act in ways that surprise you.

But the stunningly good news is that only God is perfectly good. Only God is sovereign. Only God will remain faithful to a promise. Only God can lead you to safety. Only God will give you the true delight your heart desires.

When you come to the Bible meekly and humbly, you are admitting what God says is true. We are all sinners. We are all rebels. We are all foolish. None of us seeks after God on our own. No human being can earn salvation. All man's efforts to save himself are disgusting to God. (We will learn about meekness in chapter 4.)

Conversely, all the good things the Bible says are also true! God is infinitely valuable, infinitely loving, and infinitely just. He is holy, which means He is beautiful, perfect, set apart, and completely different from fallen humanity. Astonishingly, the

Bible encourages us to expect great things from our great God, because the more we rely on Him, the more He is glorified in us (Psalm 50:15). The Bible defines true greatness as knowing God and living each day in fellowship with God (Jeremiah 9:23-24).

The spotlight of the Bible is always on Jesus, the second person of the Trinity, fully God and fully man. Looking at Jesus is the delight of every Christian, once we start to believe the Bible. Jesus is not only in the spotlight, but He is also the Word made flesh. He is the fulfillment of every promise, the perfect fulfillment of the law of God, and the complete sacrifice needed to satisfy the wrath of God that we deserved. Every human being is made in the image of God and is precious to God, yet all are sinful and flawed and need salvation. Psalm 107:20 is a wonderful promise of how God heals us through Jesus, "He sent out his word and healed them, and delivered them from their destruction."

I pray that you accept this challenge right now. When you open your Bible, pray, "God I believe your Word, and I will listen and obey and trust You. I want the wisdom of God, and I reject the man-made wisdom of this world. Only You can heal me." You are surrendering your "right" to question God's authority and His worthiness to command you. Surrender is difficult, and often it feels painful, but it is the only way to true freedom.

You will still ask God many questions, as did the psalmists: How long, O Lord? Why? Where are You? But you will also sense a new power in your life and a new hunger for the Bible. You will soon see the word of God is your life, is more necessary than bread or water or air. Instead of looking at the Bible as a vitamin supplement you should take daily—but may forget—you will see it as it really is. It is the essential medication that gives you life, freedom, joy, and salvation, instead of death and eternal separation from God. When you mess up and experience guilt and shame, you naturally want to run away from God because of His holiness and perfection. Only by reading the Bible can you see that God welcomes you just as you are into His holy place through Jesus, and you never need to run away from Him again.

I used to think I could fix my own sins. I would try to clean myself up before I would try to approach God. My prayer life and Bible study would stop when I was living in my sinful habits, and I felt ashamed. Sometimes I would try to forget God, or like Jonah, I would run away from God. Then God in His mercy would remind me that He is so different from me, and He would draw me back to Him. God's ways are so different from our ways, because He has provided forgiveness already if we only ask for it (Psalm 32:8).

Go back and read the verses at the beginning of the chapter and pray for God to speak to you right now. We were born in foolishness, but we do not have to stay fools because God is the infinite source of wisdom that we need. Jesus is our true food, our true bread, our true life. "I am the living bread that came down from heaven. If anyone eats of this bread, he will live forever. And the bread that I will give for the life of the world is my flesh" (John 6:51). God's Word is sent out for you to find it, delight in it, and see the glory of God.

Speak, O Lord by Keith Getty and Stuart Townend

Speak, O Lord, as we come to You to receive the food of
Your Holy Word.
Take Your truth, plant it deep in us shape and fashion us in
Your likeness that the light of Christ might be seen today in
our acts of love and our deeds of faith.
Speak, O Lord, and fulfill in us all your purposes for your
glory.

Teach us Lord, full obedience, Holy reverence, true humility.
Test our thoughts and our attitudes in the radiance of Your
purity.
Cause our faith to rise, cause our eyes to see Your majestic
love and authority.
Words of pow'r that can never fail, let their truth prevail over
unbelief.

Speak O Lord, and renew our minds help us grasp the heights
of Your plans for us.
Truths unchanged from the dawn of time that will echo down
through eternity.
And by grace we'll stand on Your promises, and by faith
we'll walk as You walk with us.
Speak, O Lord, till Your church is built and the earth is filled
with Your glory.

CHAPTER 3:

The Dry Riverbed of Perfectionism

"To you, O LORD, I lift up my soul.
O my God, in you I trust; let me not be put to shame;
let not my enemies exult over me.
Indeed, none who wait for you shall be put to shame;
they shall be ashamed who are wantonly treacherous.
Make me to know your ways, O LORD; teach me your paths.
Lead me in your truth and teach me, for you are the God of my salvation;
for you I wait all the day long.
Remember your mercy, O LORD, and your steadfast love, for they have been from of old.
Remember not the sins of my youth or my transgressions;
according to your steadfast love remember me,
for the sake of your goodness O LORD!
Good and upright is the LORD; therefore he instructs sinners in the way.
He leads the humble in what is right, and teaches the humble his way.
All the paths of the LORD are steadfast love and faithfulness,
for those who keep his covenant and his testimonies.

For your name's sake, O LORD, pardon my guilt, for it is great.
Who is the man who fears the LORD?
Him will he instruct in the way that he should choose.
His soul shall abide in well-being, and his offspring shall inherit the land.
The friendship of the LORD is for those who fear him,
and he makes known to them his covenant.
My eyes are ever toward the LORD,
for he will pluck my feet out of the net.
Turn to me and be gracious to me, for I am lonely and afflicted.
The troubles of my heart are enlarged; bring me out of my distresses.
Consider my affliction and my trouble, and forgive all my sins.
Consider how many are my foes, and with what violent hatred they hate me.
Oh guard my soul, and deliver me!
Let me not be put to shame, for I take refuge in you.
May integrity and uprightness preserve me, for I wait for you.
Redeem Israel, O God, out of all his troubles."
- Psalm 25

Perfectionism is widespread in our culture. We think expecting perfection from ourselves and others makes us all better and stronger. But then we criticize ourselves when we fail to meet these perfect standards. I know this drive well from my heritage. I am an Egyptian female, where our honor/shame culture teaches us to fear failure more than death. I am also a general surgeon, who learned to push myself beyond my limits to practice the art of surgery. There were very few women in my surgery training program, but I realized that I held the female residents under me to a higher standard than the males because of my own perfectionism.

My story is not a success story because this ambition and perfectionism wreaked havoc on my life, even if it seemed outwardly productive. My husband and kids suffered due to my discontentment with their best efforts which fell below my perfect standards. One of my beloved coworkers even took her own life because of her lifetime of perfectionism. This is a deadly disease that ruins lives, all because we are deceived into thinking we will make ourselves better. We saw our thirst for God in chapter 1, and the Bible being our source of life in chapter 2. Perfectionism is like a dry riverbed that can never satisfy us. It is easy to see perfection as a safe place to live where there is no need for help, and no room for criticism in a perfect world. However, pursuing perfection is a dead end because it is impossible in this life, and we cannot avoid criticism and weakness, even with our best efforts. This chapter will demonstrate the crushing burden of perfectionism so that we will never try to carry it again.

My perfectionism began when my own heart deceived me into thinking that what I was doing was pleasing to God because of my shallow reading of Matthew 5:48, "You therefore must be perfect, as your heavenly Father is perfect." These words were spoken by Jesus Himself during His Sermon on the Mount. But the context completely changes the actual meaning of this verse. Earlier in Matthew 5:20, Jesus said, "For I tell you, unless your righteousness exceeds that of the scribes

and Pharisees, you will never enter the kingdom of heaven."
Jesus' point in the sermon is that no human being can be good
enough to meet God's standard. God's standard is holy perfection. Jesus showed us that in God's eyes, the angry outburst is
as serious of an offense to His perfect standard as murder. The
lustful thought is as serious as the act of adultery.

Now clearly, Jesus is not saying that we might as well murder
and commit adultery since we all have had sinful thoughts. He
is trying to wake us up from our sinful self-righteousness and
comparisons to "those awful sinners over there" so that we
can see our own wretchedness, our own brokenness, our own
rebellion and wickedness against our perfect, holy, righteous
God. God's assessment of our sin is accurate: we are far worse
than we ever thought. The correct response to the Sermon on
the Mount is "Lord, save me" instead of trying to check off our
strengths and weaknesses. We need Jesus' perfect righteousness to stand before a holy God without fear of judgment.

Romans 3:20 became a critically important verse in my life,
illuminating my perfectionism and sending it scurrying like
a cockroach when the light turns on in a dark room: "For
by works of the law, no human being will be justified in his
sight, for through the law comes knowledge of sin." There is
no getting out of this one! We will never earn our standing
with God through our works. You and I obviously fall into the
category of human being, yet we foolishly live in ways con-
trary to this truth when we embrace perfectionism. Paul goes
on to describe our new righteousness, our perfect record in
Christ, received as a gift of grace. "But now the righteousness
of God has been manifested apart from the law, although the
Law and the Prophets bear witness to it—the righteousness of

God through faith in Jesus Christ for all who believe. For there is no distinction: for all have sinned and fall short of the glory of God, and are justified by his grace as a gift, through the redemption that is in Christ Jesus, whom God put forward as a propitiation by his blood, to be received by faith. This was to show God's righteousness, because in his divine forbearance he had passed over former sins. It was to show his righteousness at the present time, so that he might be just and the justifier of the one who has faith in Jesus" (Romans 3:21-26).

God's forgiveness, justification, and grace are the end of shame in our lives! We can finally see the truth that God does not expect us to be perfect. He expects us to come to Him empty-handed and receive grace. Our identity is then completely changed in that moment, so that the All-Powerful, All-Knowing God of the universe now sees us in Christ His Son, clothed with the perfect record of Christ. That is why the psalmist can say, "Indeed, none who wait for you shall be put to shame, they shall be ashamed who are wantonly treacherous" (Psalm 25:3). When you read the Bible and you are a believer in Christ, you are now one of the righteous because of this mighty gift of grace that you do not deserve or earn (see next chapter).

Trying to create a perfect record on your own is foolishness. Do you hate to fail? Do you always feel disappointed with yourself and others? Do you often worry about measuring up? Do you feel guilty when you need to rest? I can tell you from my life experience that this is not a healthy way to live, and it is not what God wants from your life. Jesus would not have had to come and die for you if you had things covered without Him. Let your desire for perfection and holiness drive you to drink from God's river—Jesus the living water—rather than look for your own river which is so dry.

If you are struggling with shame, look at God offering you complete forgiveness and ask Him to help you forgive yourself. Jesus took all our shame on the cross and gives us His worthiness. Picture God holding your face in His hands, looking into your eyes, and saying that He is pleased with you because of your identity in Christ (2 Corinthians 3:18).

I love these truths! They are electrifying and powerful to change our thoughts, our hearts, and our behaviors. Read Psalm 25 and see what Christ has won for you! You are now the friend of God, and He has made known to you His covenant of grace that is completely dependent on His actions, His faithfulness, His steadfast love. It's so beautiful to receive this from Him, now and for eternity. Those who reject this infinitely valuable offer of forgiveness and friendship with God will be the ones who suffer shame and loss.

Only God is your safe refuge, your true Savior. Only God is perfect. Only God determines good and evil. Only God is the judge. Do you know how to come to Him humbly and wait for Him, lifting up your soul to Him? It's humanly impossible but made possible through the Holy Spirit inside you. You let go of your pride and control, and you pray, "Not my will but Your will be done" and "Help me see Jesus as my identity right now, not my own works or failures." Think of the cross of Jesus: He was nailed, subject to human shame, mocking, and betrayal, and He chose to suffer the wrath of God against our sin. His heart is open to you, and He offers you His friendship (see John 15). He is always listening, always faithful, and always powerful to help you in your time of need. His help may not look like you pictured it would, but when you look back you will certainly see His hand on your life.

God has such compassion for us! We are not alone in this battle. Jesus our Brother and High Priest intercedes for us. "For every look at yourself, take ten looks at Christ. He is altogether lovely."[2] Let this gospel message be your obsession, your best thought every day, and your treasure. Your healing will certainly happen, either in this life or the next. The crushing weight of shame and guilt was taken off you and put on Jesus, and now you are held safely in the perfect love of Christ. When you fully understand these truths, you will find yourself laughing more at your mistakes and weakness rather than berating yourself. Christ's love and acceptance of you is your hope, not your performance. Your weakness is where God will display His power (2 Corinthians 12:9). Your expectations of others will also change, and you will experience so much joy and delight in the loving relationships you have with God and people.

---

2 1 Robert Murray M'Cheyne, quoted by Andrew Bonar in his memoir in 1845.

All Sufficient Merit by Bethany Barnard, Bryan Fowler, Shane Barnard

All sufficient merit shining like the sun,
a fortune I inherit by no work I have done.
My righteousness I forfeit at my Savior's cross,
where all sufficient merit did what I could not.

In love He condescended eternal now in time,
a life without a blemish the Maker made to die.
The law could never save us, our lawlessness had won,
until the pure and spotless Lamb had finally come.
It is done, it is finished, no more debt I owe.
Paid in full, all-sufficient merit now my own.

I lay down my garments, any empty boast.
Good works now all corrupted by the sinful host,
dressed in my Lord Jesus, a crimson robe made white,
no more fear of judgment: His righteousness is mine.

All sufficient merit, firm in life and death.
The joy of my salvation shall be my final breath.
When I stand accepted before the throne of God,
I'll gaze upon my Jesus and thank Him for the cross.

CHAPTER 4:

How to Drink from the River:
No Earning, but Effort is Needed

"For consider your calling, brothers; not many of you were wise according to worldly standards, not many were powerful, not many were of noble birth. But God chose what is foolish in the world to shame the wise; God chose what is weak in the world to shame the strong; God chose what is low and despised in the world, even things that are not, to bring to nothing things that are, so that no human being might boast in the presence of God. And because of him you are in Christ Jesus, who became to us wisdom from God, righteousness and sanctification and redemption, so that, as it is written, 'Let the one who boasts, boast in the Lord,'"
- 1 Corinthians 1:26-30

"How precious is your steadfast love, O God! The children of mankind take refuge in the shadow of your wings. They feast on the abundance of your house, and you give them drink from the river of your delights. For with you is the fountain of life; in your light do we see light."
- Psalm 36:7-9

Have you ever had your best efforts blow up and backfire on you? I once tried to compliment my former boss on her bright red suit and shoes, but I made the mistake of comparing her to Elton John when he appeared on the Muppet Show in 1978. That was not received as it was intended. Another discouraging example was when one of my patients would suffer an unexpected complication after surgery, prolonging their recovery. I cannot predict every outcome ahead of time and cannot always explain why some things happened to some patients, despite my formidable training.

Our best efforts can lead us the wrong way when it comes to religion. The human heart naturally understands religion. If I do something good, then the higher powers will act favorably toward me, and if I do something bad, then I will suffer punishment. Religion is all about earning favor with the higher power. It's all about human effort and trying harder. This is the "default mode" of the human heart, as Tim Keller used to say. The human heart also understands boasting as well: we love to be recognized and elevated over others.[3]

The gospel is something totally different, that Jesus Christ, the Son of God, has come to earth, fully God and fully man, lived a perfect life, and died on a Roman cross to bear the wrath of God for sin. On the third day, He rose again and is seated at the right hand of the throne of God, waiting for His enemies to be made His footstool, and He returns to establish the new heavens and the new earth in which righteousness dwells. Jesus is the opposite of religion: He left His high position and took the lowest position to save us through His all-sufficient merit.

---

3   Tim Keller, *The Prodigal God: Recovering the Heart of the Christian Faith* (New York: Riverhead, 2008), 128-29.

There is no human effort in the gospel. Praise the LORD! Your salvation rests on Christ's work: Christ earned your salvation for you. Receive this gift of grace. In fact, we see that human effort to earn salvation is disgusting to God in Revelation 3:15-17: "I know your works: you are neither cold nor hot. Would that you were either cold or hot! So, because you are lukewarm, and neither hot nor cold, I will spit you out of my mouth. For you say, I am rich, I have prospered, and I need nothing, not realizing that you are wretched, pitiable, poor, blind, and naked."

So what do we do now that we have believed that Jesus is our Savior? Effort is indeed part of the daily walk with God. Our effort consists of living by faith not by sight. Melissa Kruger, vice president of discipleship programming at The Gospel Coalition, once said, "Believe to receive what you could never achieve."[4] We need to open our hands and hearts to receive grace and salvation. We need to actively seek God, glorify God, worship God, and serve God because He is infinitely valuable and worthy! We fight sin in our lives, and we proclaim the truth of Jesus to everyone in word and deed. Our boasting now is in Christ's work, not our works.

Somehow, we need to focus our efforts on living in the truth that our efforts don't earn our salvation. Living like you have earned salvation from God by your good works is the opposite of the gospel and will not save you. It leads to slavery and death (see chapter 10). Instead, focus your efforts on living in the grace you have received. Godly life flows naturally out of

---

4   TGCW24 "I AM the Bread of Life", https://www.thegospelcoalition.org/podcasts/tgc-podcast/melissa-kruger-bread-life/.

your new identity in Christ. It's a paradox but it's one Christ calls us to for full living. Here are a few steps how to do it.

First, put effort into an active pursuit of the *fear of the LORD* (see chapter 8). The opposite of the fear of the Lord is the fear of man. You cannot live in both the fear of the Lord and the fear of man (Galatians 1:10). When you catch yourself worrying about what people think of you, repent! Ask God to help you live in the fear of Him and not man. The contrast is so clear in Isaiah 8:11-13: "For the LORD spoke thus to me with his strong hand upon me and warned me not to walk in the way of this people, saying: 'Do not call conspiracy all that this people calls conspiracy, and do not fear what they fear, nor be in dread. But the LORD of hosts, him you shall honor as holy. Let him be your fear and let him be your dread.'"

I have lived my entire adult life in dread. Being a surgeon is unpredictable because I never know what will come into the ER, or even into my office, on any given day. As a "recovering" perfectionist, I was terrified of failure or a bad outcome. Dread sapped my joy, my energy, and my peace. I have had to learn about God's sovereignty and power to get up in the morning without that sense of foreboding. Yes, my life is not under my control, but I fear the LORD and I know He is all powerful, good, and holy. He cannot lie, and He cannot break a promise!

I am thankful that He is changing me and giving me hope every day. I can wake up in joy knowing that I belong to God, and He will take care of me. My day will end in victory because God always wins, even if my plans are thwarted. I pray He will change me so that my plans are more like His plans, and I see His ways are far better than my ways (Isaiah 55). So often I want to stay safe and be comfortable, but God's grand plan may force me out of my comfort zone. God's surpassing beauty, kindness, and faithfulness in the past—most clearly seen in Jesus dying on the cross for me—convince me that He is the only Person whose opinion about me matters, and I want to follow Him. I am amazed that my life of faith can bring pleasure to God, and His pleasure becomes my life goal.

Next, pursue *humility and meekness.* Meditating on meekness has changed my life in the last few years. Meekness isn't weakness. Meekness, in the biblical sense, has two aspects. First, a meek person believes everything God says is true. Like soft soil, ready to receive a seed, is the meek heart receiving God's Word: "Receive with meekness the implanted word, which is able to save your souls" (James 1:21). James also talks about the meekness of wisdom, which is receiving God's truth and rejecting man-made religion, man's "wisdom." It is not possible to dabble in both types of wisdom. That is called double-minded living, or existing with one foot in the boat with God and one foot on the dock with the world. That is a very unstable place to be (James 1:5-8)!

Second, meekness involves waiting on God for His vindication. Think of Jesus, who was unjustly accused and executed on the cross by wicked men. First Peter 2:23 is the best summary of Christ's meekness: "When he was reviled, he did not revile in return, when he suffered, he did not threaten, but continued entrusting himself to him who judges justly." How different this is from our natural tendency to rise in self-defense, self-justification, and self-preservation! My pride and self-righteousness are the root of my indignation and anger at criticism. It's worth tears of repentance, especially when I see how far from Christ's heart I have strayed.

Now that I am on the meekness lookout, I see it as the most beautiful trait in someone. Sometimes we must speak out in self-defense, but before jumping into the boxing ring, ask God if this is what He wants from you right now. Sometimes He is glorified by silence, by faith in trusting Him, by waiting for His vindication. Psalm 141:3 was my prayer at many tense meetings in my career: "Set a guard, O LORD, over my mouth; keep watch over the door of my lips!"

Let's pray that God will get the maximum glory in our lives! Think of the ten plagues in Exodus: why didn't God just save the Israelites after one plague? He was getting the maximum glory and teaching us essential lessons of faith. Yet often the cost of glorifying God is giving up our desire for efficiency, ease, and comfort. Let's sacrifice these desires on the altar and give God our praise as we patiently wait for Him. First Corinthians 1:26-30 above reminds us of this paradox that God's wisdom and power are very unlike human standards. God takes away all our sources of boasting in ourselves so that we will boast exclusively in Him, giving Him the maximum glory of our lives as we delight in His greatness.

The next effort God wants us to adopt in our daily practice is *actively dying to our flesh*. This is called "mortification of the flesh" and is present in my favorite passages of Colossians 3, Galatians 5, and Romans 8. This painful process is the only way that we will grow in the fruit of the Spirit (see also chapter 9). When we are praying for ourselves and others, it is powerful to pray that we will die to ourselves and live in the power of the Spirit. We die to our pride, to our selfishness, to our desire to see our way, our kingdom come, and we humbly accept Christ's will, Christ's way, Christ's power in our lives.

Do you ever wonder if you would stand up for your faith in a life-or-death situation? What if your loved one were in danger of death unless you denied your faith in Christ? I have learned that I need to practice now, daily, dying to myself, so I'm ready whenever I am called to physically die. Exercising our faith is like building a muscle, so start small and add more challenge every day. Jesus is worth it, but only our eyes of faith will be able to see that. As we die to our flesh, our eyes will open to Christ's infinite value and the treasure we have in Him. Take all thoughts captive to Christ. Don't listen to the devil's and the world's lies. I think we all have a radio in our minds, and we choose what station we listen to and at what volume. Tune in to "Holy Spirit Radio" and the truth of Jesus, then turn up the volume. Unlike human on-air personalities, the Holy Spirit is 24/7 open to us. Reach out! Ask God to help you in your struggle, and phone a friend if you can't change the station yourself.

Finally, our fourth daily effort is to *praise the Lord*. Offer the sacrifice of praise, the fruit of your lips. Worship more, worry less. See how safe you are in Christ and celebrate the healing that has already happened. Make it your goal to boast in the cross of Jesus, not in yourself. See chapter 11 for ways to worship and praise the Lord.

Practicing these skills will not backfire on you. You will delight in the fear of the Lord, humility and meekness, dying to your flesh, and worship. You will marvel when people tell you that they see Jesus in you. Your heart will rest safely in God's unconditional love and grace. Sanctification, the process of becoming more holy like Jesus, is the result of these skills. As the verses above state, Jesus Himself has become our sanctification. You can now boast in Jesus with great joy and confidence, drinking deeply of the delight of your relationship with God, motivated by His love and beauty.

Our Pleasure and Our Duty by John Newton

Our pleasure and our duty, though opposite before,
since we have seen His beauty are joined to part no more.

To see the law by Christ fulfilled and hear His pardoning
voice,
transforms a slave into a child, and duty into choice.

CHAPTER 5:

How Drinking from the River Moves Us from Offense to Honor

"Having purified your souls by your obedience to the truth for a sincere brotherly love, love one another earnestly from a pure heart, since you have been born again, not of perishable seed but of imperishable, through the living and abiding word of God; for

'All flesh is like grass
and all its glory like the flower of the grass.
The grass withers,
and the flower falls,
but the word of the Lord remains forever.'

And this word is the good news that was preached to you. So put away all malice and all deceit and hypocrisy and envy and all slander. Like newborn infants, long for the pure spiritual milk, that by it you may grow up into salvation- if indeed you have tasted that the Lord is good. As you come to him, a living stone rejected by men but in the sight of God chosen and precious, you yourselves like living stones are being built up as a spiritual house, to be a

holy priesthood, to offer spiritual sacrifices acceptable to
God through Jesus Christ. For it stands in Scripture:
'Behold, I am laying in Zion a stone, a cornerstone, chosen and precious, and whoever believes in him will not be
put to shame.'
So the honor is for you who believe, but for those who do
not believe,
'The stone that the builders rejected has become the
cornerstone,'
and
'A stone of stumbling, and a rock of offense.'
They stumble because they disobey the word, as they were
destined to do."
- 1 Peter 1:22-2:8

I hate starting over. I like to be efficient and productive, and
starting over seems like a waste of precious time and energy. I
learned this about myself by watching tennis. When my favorite male player would win the first two sets, I would be elated,
expecting a swift win with the third set. Often, however, the
player would then lose a set. I would think that was an unfor-
tunate setback, which could be overcome for the win.

Then sometimes he would lose the fourth set, forcing a fifth
and final tiebreaker set. This to me was outrageous. How did
he allow this to happen? I realized that if I were the player I
would just give up right then. Starting over to me was just
like losing. After all that time and effort, now he was back
to square one. I always admired the player's composure and
perseverance even with thwarted plans, obstacles, and unexpected losses.

This year many of my plans have been thwarted because of my career change. My interpretation of my life situation left me more discouraged and offended than the situation warranted. God was moving me to something better, but I was upset because I had to start over. I wanted God's plan for my life to be efficient, predictable, and logical. I realize now that I was too attached to my expectations and too easily offended because of my own self-centeredness. I wanted the world and everyone in it to revolve around me. This chapter is about letting go of false ideas and offenses that hinder us from drinking from the river of delight and receiving instead real honor and security through Jesus.

Our culture teaches us to find offense anywhere we can. Think of offense as the emotion we experience when we perceive someone is impinging on our right to our own space or hurting us emotionally or physically. Handling conflict well is a lost art, because we prefer isolation without conflict over relationship with conflict. In our desire for safety over risk, we cancel anyone we perceive as a threat.

Lately, I find that resentment and offense are impossible to let go of without divine help. When I am disrespected, overlooked, or harmed, my heart adopts defense mechanisms to survive. I think negative thoughts about the offender. I long to hear of them failing, struggling, or losing, so that I feel justified. I keep rehearsing their wrongdoings against me every time I think of them so that I can continue in my malicious thoughts. I want to recruit other people to agree with my negative assessment. What an oppressive, crushing space! Here is the opposite of abundant life and drinking from the river of delight.

Isolation and discord are not God's will for our lives. God Himself is the beauty of relationship, since He is Trinity: Father, Son, and Holy Spirit. This relationship existed before He created the world. The Trinity, an essential doctrine of Christianity, is proof that loving relationships are the meaning of life, the beautiful broad space of healing and delight. As the Father, Son, and Holy Spirit live in loving relationship with one another, They created us with the glorious plan to bring us into this loving relationship as joyful recipients of God's love. Between the three Persons of the Trinity there is always love, glory, submission, and joyful celebration, much like a dance. "Each of the divine persons centers upon the others. None demands that the other revolve around him. Each voluntarily circles the other two, pouring love, delight, and adoration into them. Each person of the Trinity loves, adores, defers to, and rejoices in the others. That creates a dynamic, pulsating dance of joy and love."[5] God the Father sent Jesus to be our Savior by the power of the Spirit, to bring glory to God, and to show us His goodness and grace for all eternity. We are now united to Christ, and God sees us in Christ as Ephesians 2:6-7 states: "And raised us up with [Christ] and seated us with him in the heavenly places in Christ Jesus, so that in the coming ages he might show the immeasurable riches of his grace in kindness toward us in Christ Jesus."

Drinking from the river of delight happens when you experience the joy of the Trinity in your own life. You step into the ever-flowing waterfall of love, glory, and honor that is always present between the Father, Son, and Holy Spirit. You can always at any moment drench yourself in it because you are now

---

5   Tim Keller, *The Reason for God*, (New York: Dutton, 2008), 215.

welcomed into that new space. Jesus prayed for all believers in Him in John 17:21-23, "that they may all be one, just as you, Father, are in me, and I in you, that they also may be in us, so that the world may believe that you have sent me. The glory that you have given me I have given to them, that they may be one even as we are one, I in them and you in me, that they may become perfectly one, so that the world may know that you sent me and loved them even as you loved me."

When we realize that life is all about the *glory* of God, we see the Bible telling us a story of God's infinite grace and love in giving us this indescribable gift: Jesus. He came to save people who, by their rebellion and hatred of God, were trying to steal His glory for themselves. He came to make us people who love and worship God and live for His glory.

He came to show us how to be truly human, living in complete dependence on God. We belong in the safe place of love and harmony with the Trinity. When we enter that safe place, we see how petty and childish our hearts have been to hold a grudge or resent another person. We are accepted, loved, and honored in Christ, so we do not have to seek our own vindication and revenge. We can trust that God is the judge and leave that up to Him.

The passage above in 1 Peter is rich with gospel truth that can transform us. Everything you can see with your eyes is passing away and has no lasting glory. Only the word of the Lord remains forever. You need eyes of faith to see this invisible reality and to taste that the Lord is good. You need the divine revelation that only He is infinitely valuable. This message is exclusive. You cannot worship God and something else. You cannot have Jesus and the world. You must build your entire life on this rock, this truth, this person. There is offense, stumbling, and disobedience for those who do not believe.

There is *honor* for those who believe.

How can we move our hearts to love, worship, and obey Jesus? Where do we get the power to live in a different way? We need to see Jesus: He was chosen and precious. He promises us honor and no more shame. How did He accomplish this for us? By leaving His place of honor and taking the lowest place of rejection, dishonor, and shame on the cross.

Repent of seeking honor elsewhere. Repent of loving your comfort, and your own glory more than you love Jesus. Repent of trying to save yourself by being good. Rise up in faith and joy that He is the most glorious, the most excellent God, who offers you new life. We are now built together with other believers on the foundation of Christ. Peter describes how our words and our priorities will change because of our new identity (see chapter 9 for more on living in community).

Jesus offends us by showing us our helplessness, our need for Him. We are blind and lost and unable to save ourselves. We are foolishly running to worldly pleasures and pursuits to fill us up, things that can never satisfy us. We can be disappointed with His plans for our lives and the circuitous path He sometimes leads us on. He comes close and asks us, "Do you want to be healed?" (John 5:6)

What is your response? It takes courage to say, "Yes, Lord!" So often we reject his invitation, and we believe that life is good apart from God. Truly every good gift comes from God, and He is the author and definition of good. As Jesus said to the rich young ruler, "Why do you call me good? No one is good except God alone" (Mark 10:18). Jesus is God, so He is the definition of good!

Peter quotes Psalm 34 when he tells us to taste and see that God is good. Let's keep tasting, because we only experience how something tastes if we eat it. This is a continuous, daily habit we need to form. Whenever your mind is overwhelmed, or your heart is anxious, fearful, or wounded, turn your eyes to Jesus. Think of God's goodness, and let your heart be moved to love your Savior again. Be furiously obsessed with Jesus! Let your thoughts be about Jesus' power, glory, majesty, and love, and not about negative self-talk, or false assumptions that life must be efficient and productive to be good.

Storms are inevitable, just like unexpected life changes, or losing a tennis set. Picture Jesus the Rock being crushed for you so that your life can be hidden safely in Him. Storms will shake you, but your house will stand firm. You are built on the Rock of Ages. You will persevere to the end for the final win because Jesus will never fail you (Philippians 1:6). His Word guarantees that your faith will be refined and made more precious than all the gold in all the world (1 Peter 1:3-9). Worship our God of infinite grace and infinite supply of delight.

How Firm a Foundation by John Rippon

How firm a foundation, ye saints of the Lord, is laid for your
faith in His excellent Word!
What more can He say than to you He hath said.
To you who for refuge to Jesus have fled?

Fear not, I am with thee, O be not dismayed, for I am thy
God and will still give thee aid;
I'll strengthen thee, help thee, and cause thee to stand, upheld
by My righteous, omnipotent hand.

When through the deep waters I call thee to go, the rivers of
sorrow shall not overflow;
for I will be with thee, thy troubles to bless, and sanctify to
thee thy deepest distress.

When through fiery trials thy pathway shall lie, my grace, all
sufficient, shall be thy supply;
the flame shall not hurt thee; I only design thy dross to
consume, and thy gold to refine.

E'en down to old age all My people shall prove My
sovereign, eternal, unchangeable love;
and then, when grey hairs shall their temples adorn, like
lambs they shall still in My bosom be borne.

The soul that on Jesus hath leaned for repose, I will not, I will
not desert to his foes;
that soul, though all hell should endeavor to shake, I'll never,
no never, no never forsake!

CHAPTER 6:

Delight in Winning:
The Aroma of Christ in Suffering

"But thanks be to God, who in Christ always leads us in triumphal procession, and through us spreads the fragrance of the knowledge of him everywhere. For we are the aroma of Christ to God among those who are being saved and among those who are perishing, to one a fragrance from death to death, to the other a fragrance from life to life. Who is sufficient for these things? For we are not, like so many, peddlers of God's word, but as men of sincerity, as commissioned by God, in the sight of God we speak in Christ."
- 2 Corinthians 2:14-17

"God shall arise, his enemies shall be scattered;
and those who hate him shall flee before him!
As smoke is driven away, so you shall drive them away;
as wax melts before fire, so the wicked shall perish before God!
But the righteous shall be glad; they shall exult before God; they shall be jubilant with joy!

You ascended on high, leading a host of captives in your
train and receiving gifts among men,
even among the rebellious, that the LORD God may dwell
there.
Blessed be the Lord, who daily bears us up;
God is our salvation.
Our God is a God of salvation;
and to GOD, the Lord, belong deliverances from death."
 - Psalm 68:1-3,18-20

I went to public school in New Jersey. Early on, I learned that
there were winners and there were losers. It was obvious which
group was more desirable. I was usually the last one picked for
sports teams, and I remember once my desk was moved so that
the popular girls could sit together with the extra empty desk
instead of with me. That was a low point in my childhood:
feeling left out, rejected, and shamed. Those feelings were re-
awakened when my job as a general surgeon ended this year.
I felt that I was following God well, so it didn't make sense to
me why I was suffering so much rejection.

Winning is always on our minds. Winning means occupying
the top space all to ourselves, no contest. When we win, we experience elation and hope. Losing banishes us to a lower place.
Defeat and failure knock the wind out of our lungs, crushing
us with shame, taking away our space. It's possible to think of
death as the ultimate defeat of a human existence, something
we are all trying hard to avoid, something I was trying to save
my patients from as a doctor.

We all have an individual definition of winning, but there is
also an objective, outward, undeniable display of winning. For

the Corinthians in the passage above, this played out with a Roman triumph. When a Roman general would decisively win a battle, the Roman Senate would sometimes grant him a triumph, which was a dramatic, noteworthy, and unforgettable victory parade in Rome. You can see the Arc de Triomphe in Paris, and the original in Rome, commemorating these victories to this day.

These parades were not like our modern parades. In the front would be the prisoners of war, usually marching naked in chains to the jeers and taunts of the crowd. This was ultimate humiliation. The crowd would throw rotten food and garbage at the prisoners. The prisoners were being led to their death or lifelong slavery. Behind the prisoners came the spoils of war, the treasures of the conquered land. Next came the senators, the conquering general, his officers, and then the army. The entire city would shut down for the parade, and pagan temples would burn incense and make sacrifices to their gods. All the people except the prisoners would enjoy a feast and celebration. The culmination of the parade was the killing of the prisoners of war and a sacrifice of two white oxen to Jupiter in the temple so that all could participate in the bloodshed and victory.

The Apostle Paul refers to being in a Roman triumph parade in 2 Corinthians 2:14, but it seems that he may be thinking of himself as one of the prisoners of war in the front. In 1 Corinthians 4:9-13, Paul says, "For I think that God has exhibited us apostles as last of all, like men sentenced to death, because we have become a spectacle to the world, to angels, and to men. We are fools for Christ's sake, but you are wise in Christ. We are weak, but you are strong. You are held in honor, we in disrepute. To the present hour we hunger and thirst, we are poorly dressed and buffeted and homeless and we labor, working with our own hands. When reviled, we bless; when persecuted, we endure; when slandered, we entreat. We have become, and are still, like the scum of the world, the refuse of all things."

Paul was an apostle called and chosen by God, but his life was marked with suffering and difficulty. In Corinth, it was hard for the people to believe that God had really sent him because his life was so difficult. Wouldn't God protect someone He was sending? Wouldn't God prevent all that suffering if Paul was truly an apostle? If God *had* sent Paul, wouldn't he look and sound impressive? In the entire letter, Paul is demonstrating that suffering is indeed part of the Christian life and is actually to be expected (see 2 Timothy 3:12).

Paul sees himself as the aroma of Christ, and that he is actively spreading the fragrance of the knowledge of Christ everywhere. What is this fragrance? It is the fragrance of death and life. Christ's victory came through death, humiliation, and sacrifice. He is now our conquering king. We also are more than conquerors through Christ (Romans 8:37), and we are part of the conquering army of Christ. We also are called to die to ourselves, take up our cross daily, and follow Jesus. Drinking from the river of delight means finding satisfying, fulfilling life in Jesus every day. How do we live with both truths, life and death, and keep victory in mind even when we are suffering?

The answer lies in the story of Mary in John 12. When she anointed Jesus' feet with costly perfume, the house was filled with the fragrance. Mary's brother, Lazarus, died and Jesus raised him from the dead. Mary's gratitude and love for Jesus overflowed into an extravagant and socially awkward act of love in pouring out a life saving's worth of perfume onto his feet and wiping it with her hair. Jesus praised her action, knowing of His impending death on the cross and burial. In my life, in periods of intense suffering and loss, I see how I can anoint Jesus' feet with the fragrance of my life's worship. I see Him being led in shame to the cross, and I see that I can endure earthly shame, the stripping of my dreams and hopes, and even death, knowing that I am displaying His power and glory in this world. Do you cherish the fragrance of Christ? What does your life smell like? Nothing is more beautiful than this gospel message: Jesus conquered by being stripped of everything, so that we, who were His enemies, could live with Him in the honor and glory He deserves.

Paul refers to another victory parade in Ephesians 4:8, when he quotes Psalm 68:18. This time, God is the conquering general bringing His presence back to Zion, where He will live with His people. David wrote Psalm 68 when he was king of Israel in about 900 BC. He is worshiping God for His victory and sees God bringing back His enemies for slaughter so that His people can participate in the victory parade (Psalm 68:22-27). Sometimes as Christians, we feel like we are in the front of the parade, prisoners of war being led to our death in humiliation, and sometimes we feel we are part of God's conquering army, being led in triumph and honor.

Either way, when we see Christ the King, we can rejoice, because His victory is certain, and now we will participate in this cosmic, eternal win as part of the Body of Christ. Jesus has not only conquered all our external enemies, but He has also conquered the sin that lives inside us. He is our conqueror as well. All our allegiance is to Christ, and to His kingdom, which includes His followers. In chapter 9, we will unpack the importance of other believers in helping us endure and remain faithful in our trials and suffering. It is essential for us to remind one another of our certain victory in Christ. Take heart, all our suffering will lead to honor and glory beyond our wildest imaginations! "Henceforth there is laid up for me the crown of righteousness, which the Lord, the righteous judge, will award to me on that Day, and not only to me but also to all who have loved his appearing" (2 Timothy 4:8). Drink in your victory and delight in your future hope in Christ.

Allow God to heal you of any remaining fear of failure and ultimately, death. Jesus has already conquered death and liberated you from your lifelong slavery to fear. You never have to be afraid of missing out, of insignificance, or of failure, because Christ is victorious (Hebrews 2:14-18)! Relocate your victory into Christ, and you will never be defeated in this life or the next. I pray you will boast in your certain victory in Christ today. You're going to be in the victory parade, thanks be to God! Let the fragrance of Christ's death for you fill your heart with love and amazement, permeating your life with the pleasing aroma of love for God and humble obedience.

Jesus, Thy Head, Once Crowned *by Thomas Kelly*

Jesus, Thy head, once crowned with thorns, is crowned with glory now;
Heav'n's royal diadem adorns the mighty Victor's brow!

Thou glorious light of courts above, joy of the saints below,
to us still manifest Thy love, that we its depths may know.

To us Thy cross with all its shame, with all its grace be giv'n;
tho' earth disowns Thy lowly name, God honors it in heav'n.

Who suffer with Thee, Lord, below, shall reign with Thee above;
then let it be our joy to know this way of peace and love.

To us Thy cross is life and health; 'twas shame and death to Thee;
our present glory, joy and wealth, our everlasting stay.

CHAPTER 7:

Motivation to Drink Deeply from the River: Rewards are Real

"If then you have been raised with Christ, seek the things that are above, where Christ is, seated at the right hand of God. Set your minds on things that are above, not on things that are on earth. For you have died and your life is hidden with Christ in God. When Christ who is your life appears, then you also will appear with him in glory."
- Colossians 3:1-4

Somewhere in our twenty-first century Christian thinking, we have come up with the idea that to live for rewards is not a sincere or praiseworthy motive. We hope that no one will praise our work because we don't know how to humbly accept compliments. The reality is we are usually thinking about ourselves too much and how we look to others, how we are being perceived. None of these thought processes is in line with the gospel. True humility in the Bible is defined as thinking more about others than we think of ourselves. We are *commanded* to honor people who fear the Lord, who serve God, and who teach us the faith (Romans 12:10).

When we deny our desire for rewards, we can fall prey to a desire to look good to others. Worrying about how we look to others is a crushing weight we were not meant to carry. I have been working this out in my life when I leave my house in my small town in Alaska. I used to be one of two general surgeons, and most people knew me by sight or at least by name. Now that I am not working as the town's surgeon, I wonder what they think of me.

But God is teaching me to repent when I try to live for man's glory so that I can seek His glory. Every day, I can live out John 6:44: "How can you believe, when you receive glory from one another and do not seek the glory that comes from the only God?" I realize that I miss receiving man's glory because I do not know how to seek God's glory.

Rewards in the Bible are frequently used to motivate us to godly living. Jesus said, "And your Father who sees in secret will reward you ... But lay up for yourselves treasures in heaven, where neither moth nor rust destroys, and where thieves do not break in and steal. For where your treasure is, there your heart will be also" (Matthew 6:18, 20-21). Rewards can train a dog or a child—and our hearts too!

So how do we rightly think about rewards? Will understanding rewards change our behavior? The concept we need to understand is the abundance versus scarcity mindset.

In Alaska, we frequently run out of many fresh produce items due to supply chain issues. Often, I invest in unripe avocados, hoping that fresh guacamole may be in my future. The window of avocado ripeness is about 24 hours, after waiting for five to seven days from purchase date. Many times, I have been in urgent need of cilantro for my precious guacamole. At our store, cilantro is on the top shelf and can be seen from a long distance. Imagine I enter the store and see that the shelf is empty except for one small bunch in the corner. I pick up my pace and then in the corner of my eye, I see someone else walking to the cilantro shelf. I pick up my pace again, and they pick up theirs, and it turns into a race. What should I do when we both reach the shelf at the same time? Clearly, they want the last bunch as well! Who gets what they need and who goes without?

Now imagine the same scenario, but the shelf is full of fresh, green cilantro. It will be easy to say, "Please, you go first. Take all you need."

Living out the truth of Philippians 2:3, "Do nothing out of selfish ambition or vain conceit, but in humility count others more significant than yourselves," is much easier if the shelf is full. That is the key to the Christian life of humility: the shelf is full! Retrain your eyes to see the abundance we have in Christ, meeting all our needs, giving us joy, securing our position of honor in the family of God for all eternity. The invisible, spiritual reality of abundance is more real than the visible world around you which screams scarcity to your soul.

I am retraining my mind to see my worth in Christ's righteousness, Christ's perfect record, Christ's mighty work. I am safe and hidden in Christ. I can locate myself in Him. I have nothing to prove to anyone. He is my treasure, my reward, my identity. Think of the infinite beauty we have in Christ! As I look to Him and pray, "Jesus, You must increase, and I must decrease," I become more like Him, and His beauty radiates from me to others. This is the power of our rewards. I look at everything in my life, and I am ok with losing reputation, money, status, or fame, because I get Christ in return, and eternal glory and honor with Him in heaven.

So we can safely say that we live for rewards, because more of *Christ* is my reward. I inherit Christ and everything else! His glory is my life goal, and in the end, I will appear with Him in glory, because He is my life. This is a transformational truth. Meditate on it, and God will release His power in you, so that the world, which is passing away, will pale in your view, and Christ, who is eternal, will occupy your heart, mind, and thoughts.

Picture your life hidden in Christ and see how being in that safe space protects you from any threats around you. No one can eternally harm you, because Christ is surrounding you. His delight and approval of you helps you when you are rejected by others. Because He knows your name, you are famous in heaven.

Thinking of your union with Christ is the best thought of the day. You are welcomed into His arms forever. His love for you is infinite. What is holding you back from receiving this love deep into your heart? Is it your sin, or the consequences of other people's sins? Is it suffering? Do you think that you are disqualified from receiving His love? Pray these verses from Colossians 3 back to God and ask Him to show you that Christ is your life, and that you belong to Christ. Ask Him to help your heart experience the love of Christ within you and ask for the hope of glory to lighten your burden today. It isn't even worth comparing our current suffering to our eternal glory that far outweighs it all (2 Corinthians 4:16-18).

Hail, Thou Once Despised Jesus! By John Bakewell

Hail, Thou once despised Jesus! Hail, Thou still rejected King.
Thou didst suffer to release us, Thou didst free salvation bring.
Thro' Thy death and resurrection, bearer of our sin and shame!
We enjoy divine protection, life and glory through Thy name.

Paschal Lamb, by God appointed, all our sins on Thee were laid.
By our Father's love anointed, Thou hast full atonement made.
All who trust Thee are forgiven thro' the virtue of Thy blood;
Rent in Thee the vail of heaven, grace shines forth to man from God.

Savior hail! Amid the glory, where for us Thou dost abide;
We, by faith do now adore Thee, seated at Thy Father's side.
There for us Thou now art pleading, while Thou dost our place prepare;
For Thy saints still interceding, till in glory we appear.

Worship, honor, praise and blessing, Thou shalt then from all receive;
Loudest praises without ceasing, all that earth or heav'n can give:
In that day Thy saints will meet Thee, welcome Thee with grateful song;
Joyful hearts will ever greet Thee, source of joy to all the throng!

CHAPTER 8:

Delight in the Fear of the Lord: A Lifetime of Humility, Joy, and Contentment

"Thus says the LORD:
'Cursed is the man who trusts in man and makes flesh his strength,
whose heart turns away from the LORD.
He is like a shrub in the desert,
and shall not see any good come.
He shall dwell in the parched places of the wilderness, in an uninhabited salt land.
Blessed is the man who trusts in the LORD, whose trust is the LORD.
He is like a tree planted by water, that sends out its roots by the stream,
and does not fear when heat comes, for its leaves remain green,
and is not anxious in the year of drought, for it does not cease to bear fruit.'
The heart is deceitful above all things, and desperately sick; who can understand it?
'I the LORD search the heart and test the mind,

to give every man according to the fruit of his deeds.'
Like the partridge that gathers a brood that she did not
hatch,
so is he who gets riches but not by justice;
in the midst of his days they will leave him,
and at his end he will be a fool.
A glorious throne set on high from the beginning is the
place of our sanctuary.
O LORD, the hope of Israel, all who forsake you shall be
put to shame;
those who turn away from you shall be written in the earth,
for they have forsaken the LORD, the fountain of living
water.
Heal me O LORD, and I shall be healed; save me, and I
shall be saved, for you are my praise."
- Jeremiah 17:5-14

Many Christians do not understand the fear of the Lord, yet it
is an essential concept in the Bible. Indeed, the fear of the Lord
is the beginning of wisdom, and Christ Himself as Messiah
is said to have the "Spirit of knowledge and the fear of the
LORD" (Isaiah 11:2). We as humans instinctively understand
fear, since it is the first emotion we experience at birth, evi-
denced by our initial screams and cries as infants. Yet the fear
of the Lord is something different, more nuanced and complicated. God's forgiveness is one reason why the Bible tells us
to fear Him: "But with you there is forgiveness, that you may
be feared" (Psalm 130:4). Understanding the fear of the Lord
will lead us to the safe, healing space we need.

The fear of the Lord is what first led me to salvation. I remember when I was four years old, I snuck a cookie from the jar, and I knew that no one had seen me do it. After I enjoyed my cookie, I had the terrible realization that God saw me take the cookie. I wondered what punishment I deserved from God and what that would look like. I was terrified until I remembered that Jesus died on the cross, not for His own sake, but for my sins. Even as a small child, I wanted to be safe from punishment for my wrongdoings.

The wrath of God is a concept that is very unpopular in our culture, yet undeniably present in the Bible. God is the creator of everything you see right now, so He is the rightful owner of all. When we, as humans, as part of His creation, shake our fists at God and rebel against His ways and fail to thank Him or praise Him, we incur His wrath. We understand wrath naturally, because all of us have our own version of wrath when we are wronged, or when we do not get what we think we are entitled to. But God's wrath is perfect, righteous, and holy anger resulting in judgment. It is terrifying to behold. We can see it at this moment in part, but it will be revealed fully on the day of the Lord (Romans 1:18-32). In the book of Esther, when wicked Haman sees the wrath of the king against him, he is terrified (Esther 7:6), so how much more will there be terror in front of the King of Kings and Lord of Lords when we stand before His judgment seat (Revelation 20:11).

The fear of the Lord does involve the fear of His wrath, knowing that the greatest terror we could ever encounter is the terror of God's judgment on us. Then we turn and see Jesus, who sweat drops of blood and trembled when he saw the wrath of God looming over Him in the Garden of Gethsemane. He asked, "My Father, if it be possible, let this cup pass from me; nevertheless, not as I will, but as you will" (Matthew 26:39). Jesus Himself took the wrath of God for us, drinking every drop in the cup of wrath so that there would be none left for us to drink. As we gaze at Jesus, we see that He has defeated every enemy of our souls, and has freed us from the fear of death, and the fear of God's wrath. The crushing weight is gone, and we are free.

What does the fear of the Lord look like for the believer in Christ? It is putting God and His word in the highest place in our lives. He is the highest authority; He is our way, truth and life. We do not "fear" anything else: not man, not death, not shame or disgrace. God is awesome, we revere Him higher than anyone or anything. We repent of looking elsewhere for our wisdom, worth, purpose, or security. We see that when we have God, we have everything. We see our faith in God is more precious than all the gold in all the world (1 Peter 1:7). We see our confidence to enter the most holy place in prayer: it is all because of Christ, taking the wrath, setting us free, and giving us this secure position in the family of God. There is no place we would rather be!

Jeremiah 17 calls out two types of people: the one who trusts in man, and the one who trusts in the LORD. Those are the only two options. Trusting in yourself counts as trusting in man since you are part of humankind. Look at the stark differences between these two types of people! It's obvious which group you want to be in! Knowing that God will not break a promise will help you to know that this is *the true reality* and going to happen, whether God grants your prayer in this moment or not. Look at the wide, abundant space for the man who trusts in the Lord. It is fruitful and flourishing in all circumstances. This is where God wants you to be, daily drinking from the river of delight.

Jeremiah 17:9-10 are verses we need to memorize: "The heart is deceitful above all things, and desperately sick; who can understand it? 'I the LORD search the heart and test the mind, to give every man according to his ways, according to the fruit of his deeds.'" The sinful human heart's chief characteristic is deceit. So please don't "follow your heart" or "live from your heart!" Only the Lord understands your heart so go to Him. I have learned, when I am experiencing a strong emotion—like anger, fear, or anxiety—to take a deep breath and preach to my own heart. I say, "Janet, you are safe in God because of Jesus! You have everything you need for life and godliness. You are exactly where God wants you in this moment, so don't wish to be anywhere else, but be content. God will always show you what He wants you to do when you wait on Him. Put your trust in God alone, not in yourself or in mankind." Relocate your story into this bigger narrative of God's work in the world, and you will feel trust and faith rising in your moment of need.

Now we can see how humility, joy, and contentment are possible in any and every situation in this life. What rest there is in knowing that Jesus has forever removed God's wrath from us, and we have His perfect, righteous record instead. We can rest in Christ's finished work rather than be resentful when our work is difficult. We can care for others rather than compare ourselves to others. We have compassion for others and even ourselves, seeing Christ's compassion for us. We want to

cultivate others in Christ rather than control them.[6] We worship God in his limitlessness, and do not push ourselves beyond our limits. We rejoice in our calling and repent of discontent and our fear of missing out. God is infinitely great, so
we don't worry if what we are doing is great enough: it's our
calling from God that already makes us great. In His time, in
His strength, in His way, He will lead us to the good deeds He
has for us to do for His kingdom, His glory (Ephesians 2:10).

How do we grow in humility? We ask for it! We repent of
pride. We meditate on Christ's humility and beauty. We ad-
mire humility in others. See the pattern: humility always results in *glory* in the end (Philippians 2:1-11). Redefine a suc-
cessful day as one in which you glorified God and worshiped
Him. Failure is failing to glorify God and worship Him. If you
are failing, repent, then rise up in faith and joy, experiencing
God's delight in you as you delight in Him.

Humble living is easier when you see you are in God's safe
space for you, and everything you need has been provided.
What scarcity do you worry about today? Can you see God's
abundance instead? Keep reminding yourself that the shelf is
full (see last chapter), then put others' needs ahead of your
own. You are always welcomed into God's heart, and you can
offer that welcome to others (Romans 15:7).

Preach abundance to your heart. Instead of saying, "I don't
have enough time," remind yourself that God has given you
what you need to do what He is calling you to do today. Accept
your limits with humility and worship, because God has no
limits. Instead of calculating if you have enough resources,

---

6   Hannah Anderson, *Humble Roots* (Chicago: Moody Press, 2016), 76-77.

remind yourself that God has already provided what you need up until this point, and will continue to provide so you can do the things He called you to do today. Worship Him for His generous gifts of grace: salvation and eternal life. If you are lamenting loneliness or disappointment in your circumstances, remind yourself to thank God for His presence with you. Remember that you were once dead in your sins and enslaved to Satan (see chapter 1), but now God has made you free and adopted you into the body of Christ. Go back and read Jeremiah 17 and praise God, the fountain of living water, and the place of your sanctuary.

Nothing Either Great or Small by James Proctor

Nothing either great or small- nothing, sinner, no, Jesus did
it, did it all, long, long ago.
"It is finished," yes indeed, finished, every jot: sinner this is
all you need-tell me is it not?
When He, from His lofty throne, stooped to do and die,
everything was fully done; hearken to His cry.

Weary, working burdened one, wherefore toil you so? Cease
your doing, all was done, long, long ago.
Till to Jesus' work you cling by a simple faith, "doing" is a
deadly thing, "doing" ends in death.
Cast your deadly "doing" down- down at Jesus' feet; stand in
Him, in Him alone, gloriously complete.

CHAPTER 9:

Abundant Life in the Body of Christ

"I therefore, a prisoner for the Lord, urge you to walk in a manner worthy of the calling to which you have been called, with all humility and gentleness, with patience, bearing with one another in love, eager to maintain the unity of the Spirit in the bond of peace. There is one body and one Spirit—just as you were called to the one hope that belongs to your call—one Lord, one faith, one baptism, one God and Father of all, who is over all and through all and in all. But grace was given to each one of us according to the measure of Christ's gift. Therefore it says,
'When he ascended on high he led a host of captives, and he gave gifts to men.'
(In saying, 'He ascended,' what does it mean but that he had also descended into the lower regions, the earth? He who descended is the one who also ascended far above all the heavens, that he might fill all things.) And he gave the apostles, the prophets, the evangelists, the shepherds and teachers, to equip the saints for the work of ministry, for building up the body of Christ, until we all attain to the unity of the faith and of the knowledge of the Son of God, to mature manhood, to the measure of the stature of the fullness of the Christ, so that we may no longer

be children, tossed to and fro by the waves and carried about by every wind of doctrine, by human cunning, by craftiness in deceitful schemes. Rather, speaking the truth in love, we are to grow up in every way into him who is the head, into Christ, from whom the whole body, joined and held together by every joint with which it is equipped, when each part is working properly, makes the body grow so that it builds itself up in love."
- Ephesians 4:1-16

Relationships are difficult, uncomfortable, costly, and sometimes unpredictable. People can be mean, judgmental, fickle, selfish, prideful, or just indifferent. The older I get, the more painful relationships I can look back on, the more I hesitate to start a new one, and the more I see the necessity of them.

To bring it back to our healing space analogy, people can get into your space! They can be pushy, manipulative, and disrespectful. Disapproval can weigh us down. Loneliness creeps in when we are misunderstood and rejected.

One of the hardest aspects for me about job loss has been the loss of my work community. After working for years at the same hospital, I had a few deep relationships which disappeared when I left. I underestimated how much that community meant to me, and the grief that would creep into my space with its loss. Losing a community can be devastating, just as finding a community can be lifesaving, especially after trauma. I found comfort in my church family, and I realized how essential my brothers and sisters in Christ were to my mental health and wellbeing.

I have also experienced the pain of leaving a church due to conflict. I sometimes wonder what God was thinking when He said that Christ came to redeem a pure, spotless bride, splendid and wrinkle-free, holy and without blemish. Many times, our experiences with church and other Christians can be more like encountering Bridezilla, and we have the wounds and scars to prove it.

First, let me say that I am sorry that you have had those experiences. I am part of the problem myself being a sinner, only saved by the grace of God.

Second, I am happy to say that God clearly knew all this and that He has a good plan! There is healing and grace and we are guaranteed to win in the end! I can say this because of Christ gave himself up for the church, shedding His blood (Ephesians 5:25). Redemption is the act of buying something back, so we can safely ask, is there anything too costly for Jesus to redeem with His blood? How valuable is the blood of Jesus? Since Jesus is God, His blood is infinitely valuable. The conclusion is there is nothing that Jesus cannot redeem with His blood. There is no sin too great, no injustice too egregious, that Jesus cannot redeem its effects on your life with His blood when you come to Him in faith. He can turn anything around and make it an opportunity for spiritual growth and sanctification, making you more like Jesus in every way.

Dysfunctional relationships at church can be the result of someone else's sin, or your own sin, or a combination. Instead of spending energy figuring out the blame game, let us consider the gospel and how it relates to church conflict.

Jesus forgives everyone who has faith in Him, and "unmesses" the mess that sin has caused. We don't repent and resolve to do better because we are unable to do better on our own strength. We repent and rest in Christ, rising up in faith and joy that He will heal us because of His faithfulness! Isaiah 30:15 changed my whole perspective on repentance: "For thus said the Lord GOD, the Holy One of Israel, 'In returning and rest you shall be saved; in quietness and trust shall be your strength.' But you were unwilling . . ." Repentance means turning away from sin, agreeing with God about our sin. The willingness to repent comes from seeing God's kindness and love (Romans 2:4). But what is the *next* step? This is when we tend to make repentance about us and not about God. God wants us to rest in faith that He will heal us, not resolve to fix the problem ourselves by trying harder next time.

God is so good and gracious! He is more than able to give us a new heart, a new mind, and to put His ways into our hearts so that we love to obey. As Sam Allberry wrote "I like orange juice first thing in the morning, but I don't like it just after I have brushed my teeth. Why? The juice hasn't changed. My palate has. The presence of toothpaste changes the taste buds, and now orange juice seems horribly sour. Something similar happens as we taste God's grace in Christ. It affects our moral taste buds. Sin begins to lose its flavor."[7] So run to God when you sin and ask for forgiveness and grace. He is faithful and will do it! "Therefore the LORD waits to be gracious to you, and therefore he exalts himself to show mercy to you. For the LORD is a God of justice, blessed are all those who wait for him" (Isaiah 30:18).

---

7   Ray Ortland and Sam Allberry, *You're Not Crazy: Gospel Sanity for Weary Churches*, Apple books, (Crossway, 2023), 123.

How then do we live today in a church filled with sinners and conflict? We need the wisdom of God to know when we should stay at a church and work out our differences in love, and when we are better off at a different church. I think of Paul and Barnabas parting ways in Acts 15 over a disagreement as an event ordained by God to move the gospel to even more cities. Most of the time, the right answer is to stay and work it out. The two competing principles that every church is balancing are the purity and unity of the church. Purity means good doctrine, correct Bible teaching, and maintaining church discipline for ongoing sin issues. Unity means loving one another and accepting one another with grace and forgiveness. Insistence on purity means sacrificing unity. Insistence on unity means sacrificing purity. Both are essential. That is the razor-sharp line our churches are walking on, and we must seek God's wisdom and guidance for each situation.[8]

Ephesians 4 is a wonderful chapter to read and memorize so we can find life in the body of Christ. We are following Christ our King, who is sovereign (verse 1), humble (verse 2), conquering (verses 7-12), and patient (verses 2, 13-16). We live in a manner worthy of our royal calling from Christ when we follow these commands. Notice the order: we receive the gift of salvation and our calling first, then our changed behavior flows out of our new identity in Christ.

Sovereign. Paul was a prisoner in Rome when he wrote Ephesians, yet in Ephesians 4:1, he calls himself a prisoner for the Lord. Paul is acknowledging God's sovereignty over his life. God has a plan, and He is all powerful, so His plan is

---

8   Wayne Grudem, *Systematic Theology,* (Zondervan, 1994) chapter 45: The Purity and Unity of the Church.

always going to come to pass. We can see all the evil people do against us, and we can confidently say that God will use that for His plan (Genesis 50:20). No one can stop God. Let the sovereignty of God be your comfort today.

If you believe that God is all powerful, completely in control, and that He is reigning over all things, then you can live a life without fear, worry, or anxiety. He will always control all circumstances for His glory and your good. You can trust Him, even when you are suffering. You never have to experience shame or regret about your past because He is even controlling that, and all the outcomes related to your bad decisions. He has shed His blood to redeem your past. You can have humble, joyful confidence because you can't mess up your own life in the end. God won't let you. You belong to Him. We do have choices (see next chapter), but we understand our own inability and helplessness, and that our Savior is strong and mighty. The grace God shows us in our struggle against sin is the same grace He shows our fellow believers, making church conflict a grand opportunity to display God's grace.

Surrender to the sovereign God because He alone is worthy of your life. You can rest in the fact that there is no Plan B for your life. Your good and bad decisions are both being used to fulfill God's plans. Aim for good decisions of course, but God is so big that your bad decisions will be used for your good in the end. Your brokenness and weakness are how God displays His glory to the world! You can give up trying to control everything because only God is sovereign and in control. He is holy, holy, holy, completely unlike us. He does allow suffering to happen to those He loves. We cannot understand Him completely, so whenever your heart is filled with questions, look at the cross of Jesus. When all appears to be hopeless and lost, think of the day after the crucifixion. Surely that was what all the disciples were feeling on Saturday, but Resurrection Sunday came whether they believed it or not! Praise God: you can confidently wait for the Lord.

Humble. The Christian life is a quest for treasure, glory, and ultimate victory. Follow your humble King! He gave up His rights to save you, to call you His own. Let your calling sink in, giving you a new identity: the God of the universe has called your name, and said to all, for all eternity, "This one is Mine." You are His favored child, because He sought after you, and He knew you even before He created the world. He is our humble King, taking the lowest position on purpose so He could bring us with Him to the highest position. His covenant with us is fully dependent on *Him* and in no way dependent on us. Find your identity in this covenant of peace (Isaiah 54:10)!

Conquering. We saw in chapter 6 that Christ is the decisive conqueror, coming in a triumphal procession to claim His kingdom. He has given us spiritual gifts to bless the body of Christ, almost as if the gifts were spoils of war (Ephesians 4:8 and Psalm 68:18). He also wants to grow the fruit of the Spirit in our lives. Fruit grows as we die to the flesh and live in the power of the Spirit: "But I say, walk by the Spirit, and you will not gratify the desires of the flesh... But the fruit of the Spirit is love, joy, peace, patience, kindness, goodness, faithfulness, gentleness, self-control; against such things there is no law. And those who belong to Christ Jesus have crucified the flesh with its passions and desires."-Galatians 5:16, 22-24

Put off/put on is a common theme in Paul's writing, where you must strip off something if you want to wear something else. Strip off your pride, put on humility. Strip off your hatred, put on love. Colossians 3, Galatians 5, and Romans 8 contrast the two ways of living and help you see the difference between works of the flesh and the fruit of the Spirit. These chapters are powerful, and you will see changes in your life when you pray them regularly. It's also helpful to do a little self-assessment and see your progress in the fruit over time. Fruit of the Spirit come from the Holy Spirit, so you cannot force them to happen in your life just by willpower. God must produce this fruit in you, and you participate by asking Him to do it. I find it helpful to think of the fear of the Lord, humility, meekness, and dying to your flesh (see chapter 4) as the deep roots below the surface, and the fruit of the Spirit as the visible results of healthy roots.

If you're unsure how to pray for God to produce spiritual fruit, try this. Pray one verse at a time from Galatians 5, then adore God for the truth, confess to God where you fail to live these truths, thank God for His willingness to help you, and ask God to do those things in you (Here's an acronym to help you remember—ACTS: Adoration, Confession, Thanksgiving, Supplication).

Don't make the mistake of esteeming others highly for their gifts (preaching, teaching, and leading are the most obvious) but not expecting to see the fruit of the Spirit as well. Fruit is costly because it involves dying to the flesh! I have seen people operating in their gifts but neglecting the hard work of growing in the fruit of the Spirit, and the result is sin, usually public moral failure or private manipulation and spiritual abuse. Church leaders and church members who are cultivating the character traits of humility and meekness will be less likely to perpetuate church hurt. We are aiming for maturity, which involves both the unity of the faith and the knowledge of the Son of God (Ephesians 4:13), being filled with the fullness of Christ. We reject human cunning, craftiness, and deceitful schemes (Ephesians 4:14).

Patient. Christ is so patient with us. Just as He promised to present the Church to Himself in splendor as a pure, spotless Bride, each believer is also being transformed and sanctified. Maturity is His goal for you, and He never fails! Remember how you learned Christ. He spoke to you, and created faith in your heart, and He spoke peace between you and God for all eternity (Ephesians 2). Every day, we can repent of our rebellion and hard-heartedness, and He faithfully forgives us and heals us. Don't grow weary—remember your rewards!

Discipleship, or following Jesus along with other believers, involves an investment of time, effort, and heart vulnerability. We need each other to grow in our sanctification—our holiness, our resemblance to Jesus—because we all have blind spots about our sins and faults. An example from my life is my marriage. I never knew that I was so selfish and prideful and stubborn until I lived with another person in close proximity. We both had to learn compassion, grace, and kindness for one another, and humble communication about our tendency to hurt each other because of our sin nature. Having kids made our selfishness even more obvious, but I see the patience and kindness of God growing in both of us. Single people can grow in their faith as well by investing in the lives of other believers at church. "Iron sharpens iron, and one man sharpens another" (Proverbs 27:17).

Walking with Christ will also change how we speak. We can use our words to worship God and build His kingdom. We can create healing space for others and point them to God. Let's unpack what speaking the truth in love looks like in the church (Ephesians 4:15).

We as believers, are given the job of calling out good and evil in ourselves and in the world around us. This is what Jesus meant when He said we are salt and light in the world (Matthew 5:13-16). We can only do this as we learn God's definition of good and evil, and we learn to discern that difference as we mature (Hebrews 5:14).

Jesus tells us *not* to judge others in Matthew 7:1, which is completely different from "judging" between good and evil. In English, we use these words interchangeably, but the meaning is different in the Bible. Judging others in Matthew 7:1 is passing a verdict and a sentence on someone, as a judge would do in a courtroom. One caveat to this is the elders of a church have responsibility to judge (issue a sentence) for habitual, unrepentant sin in a member of the church, described in 1 Corinthians 5:9-13, in cases where church discipline is needed.

As an example that relates to all believers, if you know a Christian living in habitual sin, the Bible lovingly calls you to speak about that to them. The underlying assumption is that sin leads to spiritual death, causing a hardening of the heart, and making the person unable to delight in God. "Take care, brothers, lest there be in any of you an evil, unbelieving heart, leading you to fall away from the living God. But exhort one another every day, as long as it is called 'today,' that none of you may be hardened by the deceitfulness of sin" (Hebrews 3:12-13).

How do you do that? First, ask loving questions about their decision-making process, and what is their priority in life. Listen to them and let them know that you are not putting yourself in a higher position than they are in. Show them the beauty of Jesus, and that His Word is true! The path they are on leads to death. Tell them that they are loved and that others want to walk alongside them in their struggle. You are trying to persuade them to repent from sin and love Jesus, not beating them over the head with truth. Pray for them, that God would open their eyes and win their hearts.

Judging them, which is not biblical, would look like making assertions about their worth and coming up with their proper punishment, then implementing it. So in my example, if I said to my friend, "I can't believe you would do that! You are so terrible! You are the worst! You have no value!" then I'm passing judgment. Matthew 7:1-5 warns us against saying those type of statements because we are acting in a prideful way, ignorant of our own sinful tendencies. Similarly, if we discuss our friend's sin with others behind their back and expect the person listening to pass a similar verdict, that is called gossip. Sin is best dealt with directly, so go to the person involved first before recruiting others and the church elders to go with you to speak with them (Matthew 18:15-20). Pray for wisdom because every situation and person are different.

Isolation and indifference are not options for us in the Body of Christ. The analogy of the body speaks for itself. You can't ignore your own body and be healthy. You can't be rooting against your own body and survive. As a doctor, I treated diseases that were caused by the body attacking itself and causing significant harm and disability. I also had to convince some patients to take better care of their bodies. Similarly, you can't disregard your brothers and sisters in Christ because Christ lives in them just as He lives in you. You must be cheering for them, just as Christ is cheering for them. When you serve them, you serve Jesus Christ Himself. The whole body is joined together with Christ so that, "when each part is working properly, [Christ] makes the body grow so that it builds itself up in love (Ephesians 4:16).

Good speech is life-giving, honest, and filled with grace and truth. This is the way we "hold space" in our relationships. We bring our own struggles to the conversation, and we talk with others as if we are all at the same level. We don't look down on others, and we don't put some people on a pedestal. We value vulnerability and transparency. We don't steal from others by damaging their reputation, and we don't gloss over sin as if it didn't matter. Sin is like leprosy in the body of Christ, and it can spread and cause problems in the community. Thankfully, Jesus is the answer to our sin problem because He died on the cross. Let's be people who are quick to repent, slow to become offended, and eager to maintain the unity of the Spirit in the bonds of peace. God makes the Body of Christ our safe, healing space when we honor Him with our words and obey His word. This is how we live and love in a church full of sinners.

Go back and read all of Ephesians 4, asking God to do this work in you, changing your words and your attitude towards other Christians. By showing grace and forgiveness, we create safe, healing spaces for others, and display Christ's glory to the world. We can give generously of our time and of our hearts because we have received abundantly in Christ, drinking from His river of delight every day. Think of yourself as His body, because you do not belong to yourself anymore, and you can now glorify God in your body (1 Corinthians 6:19-20).

The Church's One Foundation by Samuel John Stone

The Church's one foundation is Jesus Christ her Lord;
she is His new creation by water and the Word:
from heav'n He came and sought her to be His holy Bride;
with His own blood He bought her, and for her life He died.

Elect from every nation, yet one o'er all the earth, her charter
of salvation,
one Lord, one faith one birth;
one holy Name she blesses, partakes one holy food,
and to one hope she presses, with every grace endued.

'Mid toil and tribulation, and tumult of her war,
she waits the consummation of peace forevermore;
till with the vision glorious, her longing eyes are blest,
and the great Church victorious shall be the Church at rest.

Yet she on earth hath union with God the Three in One,
and mystic sweet communion with those whose rest is won: o
happy ones and holy!
Lord, give us grace that we, like them the meek and lowly in
love may dwell with Thee.

CHAPTER 10:

Fight Sin with the Gospel: Envy, Discontentment, Hatred are Toxic to Drink

"Let not sin therefore reign in your mortal body, to make you obey its passions. Do not present your members to sin as instruments for unrighteousness, but present yourselves to God as those who have been brought from death to life, and your members to God as instruments for righteousness. For sin will have no dominion over you, since you are not under law but under grace." - Romans 6:12-14

"For we ourselves were once foolish, disobedient, led astray, slaves to various passions and pleasures, passing our days in malice and envy, hated by others and hating one another." - Titus 3:3

I spent the first half of my life thinking I was not too much of a sinner. I had very little patience and grace for other people's bad decisions because I thought so highly of myself. One night many years ago I was called back to work to do an emergency cesarean section on a mother who had been using drugs during her pregnancy. I was tired and unhappy and a bit outraged at the bad decisions which caused this situation, not to mention the helpless baby suffering as well.

My short drive to work was God's opportunity to speak. I felt Him nudging my heart and asking, "Janet, will you not have compassion on this woman?" I am thankful He did not give me time to reply. Instead, He dumped a bucket of compassion over my head. I felt overwhelmed with the warmth and love of God for me, and I realized that I was a sinner too, and a worse sinner than I had ever thought I was. I have known Jesus since my childhood, and yet I still sin. This poor woman did not yet know Jesus, and so how could I grumble about her sin? It was a privilege to help her that night, and at one moment I felt like I was touching Jesus Himself when I held her hand and prayed before surgery. I am so thankful for the kindness and compassion of Jesus. He chose to save sinners like me.

Have you thought about your sin today? As modern people, we really don't like talking or thinking about it. "Can't we just all get along?" "Nobody's perfect—I get it." "Why is God so angry about it anyway?"

Sadly, the biblical view of sin is so different from ours but is essential for life and freedom. Sin leads to death. I cannot say this enough. I have seen dead bodies, and I hate death. Dead bodies used to look like living people but are cold, decomposing, and unresponsive. My stomach turns when I see a dead body because what made them human and lovely is now gone. But that is what the life of sin does to people. Sin causes us to be blind, and to hate the things of God, to hate ourselves, to hate others. Pursuing sin is like running as fast as possible towards a cliff, with a blindfold on.

Satan, the enemy of our soul, knows that he can deceive us into believing a little sin won't kill us. Adam and Eve fell for that lie, and we continue to think in the same way. The first sin was the sin of doubting God's goodness and God's word. Satan convinced Eve that God was holding out on her, that He wasn't looking out for her best interest, and that she had better act now or miss a great chance to understand good and evil without God's input. Adam was there too, and they both ate from the forbidden Tree of the Knowledge of Good and Evil.

Eve succumbed to the sin of envy. She saw something she didn't have, she desired it, she took it, and she gave it to her husband, Adam. But all this led to them hiding from God in shame. Seeking our desires above obedience is the start of most sin. We think that God is holding back good from us, and we deserve better! In the heat of the moment, we pursue our desire for ourselves, but we quickly cower in shame and disgust when we realize that it can never satisfy.

Sin has deep roots. We are born with a broken, sinful nature, so sin isn't just something we do, it's part of who we are. *We are sinners.* We all have the potential to do every sin. God's common grace (every good thing God gives besides salvation) extends to all mankind, and usually prevents us from being as wicked as we could be. When we experience the painful consequences of other people's sin in our lives, we can sustain many injuries. Trauma has lasting effects on our bodies and minds. We can start to feel like we were robbed of our sense of vitality and life. We can feel disconnected from our own life, experiencing numbness instead of pleasure and connection with others. Healing comes slowly, but as God's Word changes our hearts, we can find our joy and life again in meaningful relationships, especially with other believers. Jesus came to give us abundant life, life that can never be stolen away, no matter what we have experienced in the past (John 10:10).

God extends so much grace to us when we sin, or when others sin against us. Grace is greater than all our sin! Remember the promise that He will never withhold a good thing from us when we belong to Christ (Psalm 84:11). Hold on to Romans 8:32: "He who did not spare his own Son but gave him up for us all, how will he not also with him graciously give us all things?" If God isn't giving it to you right now, then it's not good for you. And if He brings suffering into your life, you can trust that He will use it for your good and His glory.

If you are not drinking from the river of delight every day, you will feel thirsty and empty. Your next natural feeling is discontent. Discontentment is like the Israelite's grumbling. God freed the Israelites from slavery in Egypt in Exodus with Ten Plagues and the parting of the Red Sea. Even with these miraculous displays of God's power, they started to grumble every time they noticed a need in their wilderness journey. They did not respond with faith but questioned God's motives and power. They were living as if they were still in bondage—not enjoying the new freedom they had as the people of God.

Discontent is toxic and displeases God. It assumes that you know what you need better than God does, and He isn't providing it for you. Discontent doesn't spur you on to be a better, more productive person in God's kingdom. Instead, you wonder if God even cares about you, or if God is truly present with you. When you disobey God's Word or fail to trust His promises, you go back to living like a slave to sin (Romans 6:16). Repent of discontentment and pray for contentment.

Contentment is a learned behavior. Preach God's Word to your own heart if you lack contentment. You can sense God's delight and approval in you through Christ, giving you strength to do all that He is calling you to do (Philippians 4:11-13). You can enjoy God's presence with you as your greatest fellowship, making you unafraid of loneliness or others' disapproval. You can always worship God, because only God is infinitely valuable and worthy, and He is your inheritance (Psalm 73). You can treasure God's calling on your life, and your adoption into the family of God. You don't have to base your worth on your performance (Titus 3:4-7). You can trust God's plan for your life (Proverbs 3:5-6), even as you bring Him your needs, concerns, and desires, praying, "Not my will, but Your will be done." If you are obeying God and listening to Him, you can find full contentment in your present circumstances because God is sovereign. There is no better place to be than at the center of His will for your life. Contentment flows from savoring your future rewards and certain glory in heaven.

If you allow discontent into your personal space, your next logical thought is to compare your life to others. When you see someone who has more than you have, or you think someone took away something that belonged to you, you may fall deeper into the dark space of hatred. Hatred of another human assumes that you are God. You have passed a judgment and the verdict is in: they deserve your hatred. You want justice for their sins and grace for your own. Please note, the Bible is clear: you make a terrible, unjust judge especially when you are angry. "Be angry and do not sin" is followed by "let all bitterness and wrath and anger and clamor be put away from you, along with all malice" (Ephesians 4:26,31). "Know this, my beloved brothers: let every person be quick to hear, slow to speak, slow to anger; for the anger of man does not produce the righteousness of God" (James 1:19-20). Jesus tells us to love our fellow humans, even our enemies, and pray for those who despitefully use us and hurt us. We are only allowed to hate sin and the three enemies of our soul: the world (everything that opposes God), the flesh (self-righteous and rebellious behavior), and the devil.

Finally, unforgiveness is the sin with the worst consequences that you can allow in your life. Jesus said after He prayed the Lord's prayer: "For if you forgive others their trespasses, your heavenly Father will also forgive you, but if you do not forgive others their trespasses, neither will your Father forgive your trespasses" (Matthew 6:14-15). Surely this is serious! Forgiveness means that you release someone from paying you back for the wrong they caused you. You do not have to allow them to continue hurting you. You should think about talking to them about their sin. It is not loving to allow someone to sin against you, especially if there is a repeated pattern of sin. (It can be good and right to seek justice through our country's legal system if that type of sin has been committed, but that is not the situation I am addressing in this book.)

But you are called to forgive and leave final justice to God. This is impossible without the cross of Jesus. You need to see Jesus on the cross forgiving you, and then leave the person who wronged you there at the cross for Jesus to deal with. All sin will one day be righteously dealt with by God. Either God will allow His wrath to fall on the person who sinned against you, or Jesus will take the wrath for them. You are not the judge. Trust the judge: that is meekness. Another way to trust the judge is to fully receive forgiveness for your own sin. Martin Lloyd-Jones once said, "We must never look at any sin in our past life in any way except that which leads us to praise God and magnify his grace in Christ Jesus." If God has forgiven you, then stop punishing yourself for it.

I want to encourage you in this fight against sin today. You need faith and patience to keep fighting, but rest assured you will receive a great reward. Let us help one another to fight sin by confessing openly and honestly about our own struggles and praying for one another. Delight in the infinite compassion and grace for us in Christ. He is our merciful and faithful High Priest, and His blood is all-powerful. He will forgive us and cleanse us from all guilt and shame. Come into the light and find healing and hope (1 John 1:5-10). We need each other in this battle. "Therefore, confess your sins to one another, that you may be healed. The prayer of a righteous person has great power as it is working" (James 5:16).

You are not trapped by sin anymore. Jesus has conquered your sin already. You have the power to fight sin by the blood of Jesus. Allow God to change your mind with these truths: "But now that you have been set free from sin and have become slaves to God, the fruit you get leads to sanctification and its end, eternal life. For the wages of sin is death, but the free gift of God is eternal life in Christ Jesus our Lord" (Romans 6:22-23). Picture yourself being welcomed into God's large, abundant healing space where all your needs are met and infinite grace and compassion flow like a river. Realize that God dwells with His people as His "happy place" and look at what it cost Him to make your heart His home (Ephesians 2:22). You will know that you are winning the battle when you boast in Jesus and see Him as your greatest treasure.

How Deep the Father's Love for Us by Stuart Townend

How deep the Father's Love for us, how vast beyond all
measure,
that He should give His only Son to make a wretch His
treasure.
How great the pain of searing loss, the Father turns His face
away,
as wounds which mar the Chosen One bring many sons to
glory.

Behold the Man upon the cross, my sin upon His shoulders,
ashamed,
I hear my mocking voice call out among the scoffers.
It was my sin that held Him there until it was accomplished.
His dying breath has brought me life, I know that it is
finished.

I will not boast in anything, no gifts, no power, no wisdom,
but I will boast in Jesus Christ, His death and resurrection.
Why should I gain from His reward? I cannot give an answer,
but this I know with all my heart:
His wounds have paid my ransom.

CHAPTER 11:

Treasure your Treasure:
Delight in Jesus Every Day

"Do not lay up for yourselves treasures on earth, where moth and rust destroy and where thieves break in and steal, but lay up for yourselves treasures in heaven, where neither moth nor rust destroys, and where thieves do not break in and steal. For where your treasure is, there your heart will be also." -Matthew 6:19-21

"Now therefore, if you will indeed obey my voice and keep my commandments, you shall be my treasured possession among all peoples, for all the earth is mine; and you shall be to me a kingdom of priests and a holy nation."
- Exodus 19:5-6

All of us treasure something. My favorite possession is my hot tub. (I also love a beautiful necklace that my husband designed for me on our tenth wedding anniversary. But I think I love my hot tub more!) I love everything about my hot tub. I love cleaning it. I love keeping the chemicals in the right range. And of course, I love sitting in it, especially with friends and family. I love it in the snow; I love it in the rain; I love it in the sun; I love it at night; and I am in it almost every day. I am not being paid to advertise it. I just love it!

What do you treasure? I'm sure you feel the same way about it as I feel about my hot tub. When your heart is enjoying its greatest treasure, you feel content and happy. This is the secret to entering God's healing space: treasure your treasure which is God Himself. You will soon discover the amazing truth that God treasures you as well.

So how is Jesus our treasure? I can't see Jesus; I can't touch Him; and sometimes He just seems far away. This chapter will help you center your focus on Him every day so that you will treasure Him more easily. Your life will change when you do!

What tempts our hearts to treasure something more than Jesus? I can think of many temptations in my own life: money and the power and security it brings, fame and influence, beauty, and relationships. Our error lies in the ordering of our loves. Money is necessary, as are relationships, but we can easily turn them into our measure of worth and value as a human being. Only Jesus can be our treasure if we want to drink from the river of delight because only Jesus is worthy of our worship. It is sinful to worship anything other than God, and sin always leads to death.

Money may be our biggest temptation, as Jesus said, "You cannot serve God and money" in Matthew 6:24. I fight the temptation with this little mental exercise, reminding myself that there is no comparison between God and money. Think of how valuable the sun is. The sun is the source of life, warmth, light. Without the sun, the earth would freeze, and we would all die. Could you quantify the value of the sun in dollars? That would be impossible. Yet even the sun is not infinitely valuable. It is extremely valuable, but only God is infinitely valuable, because only God is the creator of the sun.

Now think that the same God who could hold the sun in His hand lives inside *you* through the Holy Spirit. Take a deep breath and think about that. Would He abandon you over a bad day or decision? Would He run from you in your hour of need? Worship Him and see how your treasure is secure. "In him we have obtained an inheritance, having been predestined according to the purpose of him who works all things according to the counsel of his will, so that we who were the first to hope in Christ might be to the praise of his glory. In him you also, when you heard the word of truth, the gospel of your salvation, and believed in him, were sealed with the promised Holy Spirit, who is the guarantee of our inheritance until we acquire possession of it, to the praise of his glory" (Ephesians 1:11-14). You have an eternal inheritance, and a guarantee of future glory because the Holy Spirit lives inside you.

Do you sometimes treasure fame? Think of Jesus' fame. Jesus, who created everything by His power, also sustains our material world, holding our atoms together on a molecular level, and keeping the universe together on a cosmic level. Now think of that same Jesus entering the world He made as an ordinary, lower-class human, living in an ordinary family, and working as an ordinary carpenter for most of his adult life. His ministry was three years long and ended in execution by Rome. All He possessed at the time of His death was a tunic.

So why did Jesus leave behind His fame and glory in heaven to live as a humble human on earth? Because our God is glorious in power, and His glory is manifested in His ability to save us. We worship the only God of salvation. So if Jesus knows your name, no one else matters. If Jesus is proud of you, you don't need anyone else's approval. It's even more dramatic than if you were at a massive concert and the lead singer picked you out of the crowd and brought you on stage and told everyone that he loved you and cherished you. Jesus has done that for each of us: "But you are a chosen race, a royal priesthood, a holy nation, a people for his own possession, that you may proclaim the excellencies of him who called you out of darkness into his marvelous light. Once you were not a people, but now you are God's people; once you had not received mercy, but now you have received mercy" (1 Peter 2:9-10). Peter is quoting Hosea here, and he is doing that on purpose.

Hosea is a memorable Old Testament prophet who was commanded by God to marry an unfaithful prostitute. Her name was Gomer. Her first child may have been Hosea's but her next two children were not. Their names were Jezreel, No Mercy (Lo-ruhamah), and Not My People (Lo-ammi). She even left Hosea after they were married to go back to prostitution until he redeemed her and brought her back again. We are like Gomer in that we can quickly turn away from God and go back to our old ways of sin, shame, and self-destructive behavior. Jesus is famous for saving sinners, of whom I am the worst (1 Timothy 1:15)! Thank you, Lord Jesus, for loving me, seeking me out, and bringing me back to this safe place of honor and glory.

Do you sometimes treasure physical beauty? Think of Jesus' beauty. He is fully God and fully man. There is a man on the throne of the universe with ten fingers, ten toes, two eyes, a nose, and a mouth. How could Jesus have been tired, hungry, and sleepy? Because He is fully man. How can Jesus be all knowing and all powerful? Because He is fully God. How can Jesus have paid the infinite price for our sins? Because He is fully God. How can God the Father see Him as our substitute and accept the sacrifice on our behalf? Because He is fully man.

Let these thoughts occupy your mind and heart and worship Him. He loves us as a bridegroom loves his bride. "Then I heard what seemed to be the voice of a great multitude, like the roar of many waters and like the sound of mighty peals of thunder, crying out, 'Hallelujah! For the Lord our God the Almighty reigns. Let us rejoice and exult and give him the glory, for the marriage of the Lamb has come, and his Bride has made herself ready; it was granted her to clothe herself with fine linen, bright and pure'- for the fine linen is the righteous deeds of the saints" (Revelation 19:6-8). Jesus clothes you with beauty by grace, and you respond with righteous deeds done by His power, for His glory, and with eternal rewards.

Do you treasure your relationships with family and friends? Jesus brings you into an eternal relationship with God! Every earthly relationship is a treasure, but none can satisfy you the way your relationship with God can. We are more than just a physical body, more than just our emotions, actions, and motives. We are spiritual beings manifested in physical bodies. As humans, we are not able to fully see one another the way God sees us. Jesus created the unseen you to know Him. He looks deep into your being and knows you to the deepest depths. Yet His love for you is infinite, and His grace is greater than all your sin and rebellion (Romans 5:20). Fully known and fully loved by God is the best relationship you can ever have, and nothing can separate you from Him (Romans 8:31-39)! Heaven begins now. We belong to the Lord, and we belong in the family of God. God will make the flawless beauty of Jesus evident in your unseen soul. You can have courage to be vulnerable and transparent with others.

Jesus was seen by all, yet was crucified and hated, so you can be seen by God, and loved and accepted. He was thirsty on the cross so you could drink the living water, the river of delight. Jesus' head was crowned with thorns as a picture of His reversal of the curse of thorns, frustration, and pain from Genesis 3. Our relationships with others will be transformed by divine strength and confidence, so when hurts and disappointments come our way, we have unshakable hope and joy in God (Hebrews 12:28-29).

Treasure this new position you have in Christ. Remember His love and show that love to others. Welcome to your safe place in Jesus' open arms, because He will never let you go.

Fairest Lord Jesus by Joseph Seiss

Fairest Lord Jesus! Ruler of all nature!
O Thou of God and man the Son!
Thee will I cherish, Thee will I honor,
Thou my soul's glory, joy, and crown!

Fair are the meadows, fairer still the woodlands, robed in the
blooming garb of spring:
Jesus is fairer, Jesus is purer, who makes the woeful heart to
sing.

Fair is the sunshine, fairer still the moonlight, and all the
twinkling starry host:
Jesus shines brighter, Jesus shines purer than all the angels
heav'n can boast.

Beautiful Saviour! Lord of the nations! Son of God and Son
of Man!
Glory and honor, praise, adoration now and forever more be
Thine!

CHAPTER 12:

Glory and Rest in Jesus:
This is Where We Belong

"So then, there remains a Sabbath rest for the people of God, for whoever has entered God's rest has also rested from his works as God did from his.

Let us therefore strive to enter that rest, so that no one may fall by the same sort of disobedience. For the word of God is living and active, sharper than any two-edged sword, piercing to the division of soul and of spirit, of joints and of marrow, and discerning the thoughts and intentions of the heart. And no creature is hidden from his sight, but all are naked and exposed to the eyes of him to whom we must give account.

Since then we have a great high priest who has passed through the heavens, Jesus, the Son of God, let us hold fast our confession. For we do not have a high priest who is unable to sympathize with our weaknesses, but one who in every respect has been tempted as we are, yet without sin. Let us then with confidence draw near to the throne of grace, that we may receive mercy and find grace to help in time of need."

- Hebrews 4:9-16

Do you feel more alive now than when you started reading this book? My journey towards life and healing and delight can inspire you and guide you insofar as you let the Word of God do a mighty work of grace in your heart. The Word of God is like a sharp sword in that it cuts deeply, swiftly, accurately, and painfully, just like a surgeon's knife. The cancer of sin and rebellion is growing inside you and needs to be cut out so you can live and heal and thrive. Here is the paradox: to find life, you must be willing to die to your flesh. To know God, you must lay down your pride and your human wisdom. To treasure God, you must value Him above all other treasures. God is the best surgeon. He wields His tools well, and His outcomes are magnificent.

Surrender to God can feel like death before it feels like freedom and rest. When I am suffering, I struggle in my present moment to sense God's abundance, God's delight, God's healing presence, until I remember this analogy. Suffering can be like a canvas on display. God is painting a picture on the canvas of my suffering of the beauty of Jesus, specifically His surrender to His Father in His moment of agony. In this moment of my suffering, I can surrender to God. My High Priest, Jesus, is sympathizing with me, and He is helping me endure the suffering with patience and faith. When people see my life's canvas with God's painting, they see Jesus in me. Glory and rest in Jesus start here.

In this last chapter, we have finally arrived at the glorious safe space that God has provided for us: He welcomes into His rest. What is this true rest, this Sabbath rest, that the Bible speaks of?

True rest has eluded us modern people. It takes more than a good night's sleep or a tropical vacation to give us true rest. We may be swimming in modern convenience and time-saving devices, but our hearts and minds rarely experience rest. We are individualists. We drive ourselves to achieve success for our own reputation and glory. We have never achieved enough. We hear an inner voice criticizing us because of our own perfectionistic standards. The curse pronounced after the fall in Genesis 3 demonstrates the fruitlessness in our work and in our rest. We experience frustration: "By the sweat of your face you shall eat bread" (Genesis 3:19).

The underlying reason for our unrest is that we have forgotten to rest in Jesus' finished work on our behalf. We all know deep in our souls that judgment is coming. God is the Judge. His standard is holy perfection. He knows everything and we are not hidden or safe on our own. He is our only refuge, and there is no refuge from His wrath apart from Jesus (Psalm 2:12). Are you living in joy and confidence in Jesus' finished work on your behalf? If not, repent! Drop anything you are holding on to and cling to Jesus. Reject the lies that you need to earn your forgiveness and acceptance. Let go of your agenda and accept God's plan today. When you let go, God gives you everything you need including obedience and faith. See Jesus alone in the garden of Gethsemane just before He was crucified, sweating blood in agony, and see that by His sweat, we receive the Bread of Life, now and forever.

The opposite of rest in Jesus is rebellion. Like the children of Israel in Exodus 17, we grumble against God, forget His promises and His goodness, and we question His Word. Grumbling and complaining against God is likened to testing the Lord.

Their question stirs up the wrath of God: "Is the LORD among us or not?" (Exodus 17:7) In their rebellion against God, they longed to return to slavery in Egypt. Today rebellion against God looks very similar in that the only other place to go is back to our former slave masters of sin and Satan's power. Instead of rebelling, remind yourself of the gospel. Jesus died for your rebellion so that God can now always be with you, and you are united to Christ. His past is now your past, His future is now your future, and He empowers you in the present to live for Him.

Enter God's rest by believing and living out His word. When you hear the word of God, do not harden your heart but receive with meekness these truths. You are welcomed into God's healing space of safety and rest by grace through faith in Jesus. You are so welcomed that there are celebrations in heaven going on right now because of your faith (Luke 15:7)! Remember your calling, and the hope you have that God chose you and rescued you when you could not save yourself. Remember how Eden means delight, and Gods' presence in Eden was what made it a delight. You are now welcomed into God's healing space, where God lives. You can experience delight today in God's presence. Your real home is with God, and while you live on this earth you are a sojourner and a foreigner whose citizenship is in heaven (Philippians 3:20).

Through Jesus we are already experiencing this rest now in part, but the kingdom of God is not fully here yet. What do we do while we wait? Hebrews 4 speaks about a Sabbath rest, going all the way back to Genesis 2 when God rested on the seventh day of creation. God set apart the seventh day so that we would learn this rhythm: work and then rest because your work is completed for the week, and you can enjoy the fruit of it in community with God and others. God is always at work, so we can lay aside our projects and agenda for a day and rejoice in God's mighty work of redemption which is ongoing. In this way, we are freed from the worship of our own productivity, and we acknowledge that God is our provider, not our own hands. We are declaring that we are no longer slaves to sin, and we live in God's kingdom, not the kingdom of this world. We worship God and enjoy the Body of Christ, His church. We tell others of God's rescue and salvation. We wait in faith for the fulfillment of God's promises and the appearing of the New Heavens and the New Earth. We pray for each other to win the battle against sin, and to drink from the river of delight in God. We relocate our identity and our boasting into Christ, because now we live in Him and He lives in us (Galatians 2:20).

I am enjoying life in God's safe healing space today. I am not writing my own story, but God is writing me into His story, which is eternally significant. When I am powerless to change my circumstances or my attitude, I run to God in prayer and read His Word. I do not have to wish I were somewhere else, or adopt unhealthy habits like avoidance, denial, blaming others, self-pity, rage, or envy. I have learned the secret to being content in every and any situation, because I can do all things through Christ who strengthens me (Philippians 4:11-13). Jesus offers us true healing, true resilience in suffering, and a new identity of being united to Him.

Don't allow any false perception of reality to steal your joy and peace. The Word of God is essential for you to properly interpret your story in light of God's bigger redemption story.

You are broken by sin, but you are not trash. God takes broken vessels and makes them even more beautiful and strong than they were before.

When I am struggling with my self-criticism of my own productivity, and my feelings of not measuring up, this analogy gives me a better perspective. God has adopted me into His family, and the family business is now mine as well. God is in the business of redemption—buying back sinful and broken people, healing them, and sending them out as His ambassadors. When I respond to His redemption in worship, I am being eternally productive! The following verses describe this new way of looking at life, and our new life mission in God's family business:

> For the love of Christ controls us, because we have concluded this: that one has died for all, therefore all have died; and he died for all that those who live might no longer live for themselves but for him who for their sake died and was raised. From now on, therefore, we regard no one according to the flesh. Even though we once regarded Christ according to the flesh, we regard him thus no longer. Therefore, if anyone is in Christ, he is a new creation. The old has passed away; behold, the new has come. All this is from God, who through Christ reconciled us to himself and gave us the ministry of reconciliation. Therefore, we are ambassadors for Christ, God making his appeal through us. We implore you on behalf of Christ, be reconciled to God. For our sake he made him to be sin who knew no sin, so that in him we might become the righteousness of God. (2 Corinthians 5:14-21)

I pray that you experience God as your safe space. I pray your heart is so moved by His love and delight in you, that you feel peace and joy as you wake up each day. You belong to Him. You are His treasure, His inheritance. Today, when you hear His voice, you can listen and obey. Your obedience brings pleasure to Him, and He turns your trials and sorrows into joy and goodness in the end. Knowing that He is writing your story gives you faith that it will all turn out well in the end. Live in the present, pray without ceasing, and the peace of Christ will guard your heart and your mind. The final Sabbath rest is coming, but today you can find rest in Jesus as you drink from the river of delight.

The Love of God by F.M. Lehman

The love of God is greater far than tongue or pen can ever
tell.
It goes beyond the highest star and reaches to the lowest hell.
The guilty pair, bowed down with care, God gave His Son to
win;
His erring child He reconciled, and pardoned from his sin.

When hoary time shall pass away, and earthly thrones and
kingdoms fall;
when men who here refuse to pray, on rocks and hills and
mountains call;
God's love so sure, shall still endure, all measureless and
strong;
redeeming grace to Adam's race- the saints' and angels' song.

Could we with ink the ocean fill, and were the skies of
parchment made;
were ev'ry stalk on earth a quill, and every man a scribe by
trade;
to write the love of God above would drain the ocean dry;
nor could the scroll contain the whole though stretched from
sky to sky.

O love of God, how rich and pure! How measureless and
strong!
It shall forevermore endure- the saints' and angels' song.

Epilogue

The Battle Goes On: If You aren't Fighting, You are Losing

This letter sums up the healing truths that I have learned from God in my season of suffering, disappointment, and uncertainty. I pray this for myself and you, dear reader, each day. We can replace negative thoughts with positive truths from the Bible with practice. May God deliver us into this broad space of healing, hope, and love through His mighty Word. The best is yet to come, and the river of delight is always flowing for you and for me.

Dear Christian Brother or Sister,

I want you to know that I am rooting for you. You have Christ living in you, the same Christ who lives in me. The faith in your heart is more precious than all the gold in all the world. You will one day reign with Jesus on this earth, a kingdom of priests to our God.

The world is pouring "self-help" down your throat all the time. The gospel of Jesus Christ is telling you the opposite, and you cannot believe both are true! Keep reminding yourself that you are unable, but God is able. You are broken by sin and limited, but God is limitless. Your heart is deceitful and not to be trusted, but God is always trustworthy and true. You are feeling defeated and helpless, but Jesus is the conquering King who is currently seated on the throne of the universe, doing all things for your good and His glory. You are a child of the living God.

You need help in this battle. You must find other brothers and sisters who can come alongside you and encourage you. Even Moses needed Aaron and Joshua to hold up his arms during a battle, and Jesus took three disciples with Him into the garden of Gethsemane to pray. Sadly, all humans will fail you at times, and you will fail them at times, so keep your eyes on Jesus who never fails.

Your job is to receive. Receive God's love for you, His infinite grace, and His forgiveness and cleansing. Take a deep breath and receive it into your soul. The invisible reality is more real than anything your eyes can see. You have abundance in Christ, everything you need for life and godliness. Try to identify the cause of your frustration or anger or despair, then release it to God and receive the better thing in Jesus. And rejoice! This activity done daily will transform your life. It's also called repentance, or turning away from your way, your will, your kingdom, and embracing God's way, His will, His kingdom, and receiving His strength.

True repentance is returning to God and resting in Christ. It's not about resolving to do better next time because you are unable to change your sin nature. You need the gospel message of Jesus to change you at the level of your heart, not just your actions. When you come to Him in repentance, you turn away from sin, back to Him, and then rise up in faith and joy that you are forgiven and that He will keep His promise to restore you and cleanse you and fix all the problems you just caused by sinning (in His way, His timing, and sometimes in the next life). Ask Him to make you hate sin and to show you that sin always leads to death. Ask for tastebuds that love grace, not sin.

There is infinite power at your disposal in Christ! Your spiritual "bank account" is full, but you need to learn how to make withdrawals so you can live as a beloved child of God, not an orphan. You do this by repentance, faith, and time with God and His people. When you are poor and needy, ask God to fill you with His Word, His presence, His Spirit. He is generous, kind, good, and patient. He has compassion for you. It's His kindness that leads you to repentance. Stop beating yourself up, because you cannot atone for your own sin. Look at Jesus dying on the cross, shedding His blood for you. There cannot be any other way to be forgiven because Jesus asked if there was any other way, and the Father said no (Luke 22:42).

When you are experiencing strong temptation, run away. Do not put yourself in situations where you know you will be tempted. If you must go somewhere with temptation, phone a friend to pray and even come with you. Bring others into your struggle. When you experience victory, celebrate with those who were praying for you. Don't let shame isolate you, because that is letting the devil win. When your thoughts are spinning out of control, or you are sucked into your phone scrolling, cry out to God, and run back to Him. He has open arms. He does not look at you with disappointment or roll His eyes at you. Celebrate that these changes are happening, that you run to God sooner and sooner!

Your three enemies are the world, the flesh, and the devil. All three are real and are out to kill you. The world wants to convince you that God is not to be trusted, that He is not the only source of good and truth. The world is opposed to God and His ways and hates God, offering you power, control, and fame instead. The flesh wants you to think that your sins aren't that bad, and that you can fix your own problems with your own strength. The flesh is self-justifying behavior, or performance-based worth, deceiving you to think that you don't really need a Savior. The devil, or Satan, is a demonic being who is actively scheming to destroy you with lies, shame, guilt, and faulty emotions. He wants you to hate others, worship yourself, and forget about God.

Your weapons of battle involve the Holy Spirit who lives inside you, the body of Christ, other believers who can stand with you, and the Word of God. Your job is to guard your heart. If you drink from the river of God's delight, you will lose your taste for sin and the world. So keep up with the "open-heart surgery" every day. Let the Word of God cut out the deep, broken parts of you and fill you with the infinite presence and power of God. Prayer can be as easy as breathing. There is no prerequisite to prayer. Come as you are and receive. God knows what you need, and He is happy to provide!

Don't be like the children of Israel in the Old Testament! When they were in the wilderness, they tested God by asking, "Is the Lord among us or not?" They grumbled. They did not see God providing for them because they didn't have eyes of faith. They were living like slaves in Egypt even though God had freed them. Keep looking at Jesus on the cross. He was forsaken so you would never be forsaken. He took all the wrath so there is not one drop left for you. He now delights in you, and eagerly awaits the day when you will be face to face, beholding His glory and seeing Him smile at you. This is the face you have always wanted to see beaming at you, proud of you, and cherishing you! It's going to happen, brothers and sisters! Be patient and wait for Him to act.

I can't wait to see you on that day, and to hear you say, "It was all worth it! Let me tell you what Jesus did for me."

All glory to God, and praise and thanks to Jesus Christ!

A Debtor to Mercy Alone by Augustus Toplady

A debtor to mercy alone, of covenant mercy I sing,
nor fear, with God's righteousness on, my person and
off'rings to bring.
The terrors of law and of God with me can have nothing to
do;
my Savior's obedience and blood hide all my transgressions
from view.

The work which His goodness began, the arm of His strength
will complete;
His promise is Yea and Amen, and never was forfeited yet.
Things future, nor things that are now, not all things below or
above,
can make Him his purpose forgo, or sever my soul from His
love.

My name from the palms of His hands, eternity will not
erase;
imprest on His heart, it remains in marks of indelible grace.
Yes! I to the end shall endure, as sure as the earnest is giv'n;
more happy, but not more secure, the souls of the blessed in
heav'n.

Personal Notes

Acknowledgments

First, I want to say thank you so much to you, my reader! This is my first time being an author, so I greatly appreciate your kindness, patience, and grace in reading until the end. I hope you will be transformed by the power of God after reading this book. God is faithful to do amazing things in your life through the reading of His Word. Don't give up—you have a lot of people cheering for you including me.

Second, my editor, Mikaela Mathews, was instrumental in coaching me on my author journey. She saw the potential in this book and helped me to rewrite, rewrite, rewrite. Looking forward to more projects together, Sister!

Third, my dear friend Voni Harris, a soon-to-be best-selling author, helped me when I was discouraged. She loves to tell stories, and she encouraged me add more of my story into the chapters. Karen Zinck, you and Voni were on the same wavelength, and I also thank you for your help and encouragement.

Fourth, I could not do this without a lot of help from my friends. I am blessed with many friends. My best Alaskan friends are Katrina Virgin and Rachel Whiddon, who stuck with me when I was down and who showed me the courage and tenacity that I love to see in others. I am so thankful for every moment I get to spend with you both. Dena Norman is my friend who always reminds me to read my own notes. Dena started me on my retreat speaking journey and I am so thankful she invited me to speak at her church ladies retreat a few years ago. My two sister-in-laws, Trisha and Juliette, are a treasure of grace to me—the sisters I always longed for but never had growing up. I also hit the mother-in-law jackpot when I got married. Thanks for faithfully being there for me, Anita! Three ladies have been my soul-sisters for my entire life: Karan Pescatore, Cathy Mersereau, and Lois Szeliga. I have some amazing cousins too: Chrissy, Sylvia, Caroline, Nevien, Christy, all courageous people who love the Lord and pray for me often. I cannot name all my friends here, but please know that I am thankful for you.

Fifth, I am thankful for all the people who have attended my Bible studies or retreats. It is such a privilege to lead you towards Jesus, and to show you the beauty of Jesus in the gospel. I thank God for His work in your lives, and I look forward to diving into God's Word with you for many years to come. Your participation in discussions is what gives me new ideas and inspiration.

Finally, I must thank the most important people in my life: my Lord Jesus Christ, and my family. Jesus found me when I was lost and dead in my sins. He rescued me and has sustained me every moment of my existence. Jesus has called me and gifted me to do His will, and that calling is irrevocable (Romans 11:29). There is no one like You, Jesus! I am so thankful that my entire family knows and loves Jesus, and I pray that all who read this book will love Jesus more, walking with Him every day from now through eternity. He is powerful to sustain us, and He will complete His good work in us (Philippians 1:6).

My husband, Dan, and my three sons are my favorite people. Thanks, Babe, for choosing to marry me, and thanks for welcoming me into your godly family. May God bless you all, as He is blessing me through you. Even though I left my parents, brothers, and extended family and friends in New Jersey a long time ago, I am thankful that they have kept me close to their hearts. I am so thankful to belong to this family, and more importantly, the family of God.

www.ingramcontent.com/pod-product-compliance
Lightning Source LLC
Chambersburg PA
CBHW031426120626
46545CB00006B/2296